Current Issues in Day Care

Readings and Resources

Current Issues in Day Care:
Readings and Resources

Edited by Carol H. Thomas

ORYX PRESS
1986

Copyright © 1986 by
The Oryx Press
2214 North Central at Encanto
Phoenix, Arizona 85004-1483

Published simultaneously in Canada

Printed and Bound in the United States of America

∞ The paper used in this publication meets the minimum requirements of American National Standard for Information Science—Permanence of Paper for Printed Library Materials, ANSI Z39.48, 1984.

Library of Congress Cataloging-in-Publication Data

Main entry under title:

Current issues in day care.

  Bibliography: p.
  Includes index.
  1. Child care services—United States—Addresses, essays, lectures. 2. Day care centers—United States—Addresses, essays, lectures. I. Thomas, Carol H.
  HV854.C87   1986   362.7'13'0973   85-43092
  ISBN 0-89774-222-2

Contents

Preface

According to the latest U.S. Bureau of the Census figures (1983), half of all mothers of children under the age of 6 are employed outside of the home.[1] This number reflects the need of nearly 9 million children for some form of day care, 3 million of whom are under the age of 3.[2] In addition, 18 million youngsters between the ages of 6 and 14 have working mothers, yet only a relatively small percentage (9 percent) of these children are enrolled in before- and after-school programs.[3] It is estimated that, by 1990, there will be a significant increase in the number of children requiring day care services, especially in the preschool age range, since mothers of preschoolers are those currently making the greatest impact upon the job market.

For the majority of working mothers, the decision to go to work or to reenter the work force is prompted by the demands of a family budget that requires 2 paychecks. There are also a significant number of single parents who are the sole source of support for themselves and their children; employment for them is an absolute necessity rather than an option. For others who have, perhaps, interrupted a career in order to start a family, the decision to return to the working world may be a personal choice. Regardless of the motivation for seeking employment outside of the home, one of the most difficult dilemmas faced by working parents is that of providing quality day care for their children.

The subject of day care is complex and multifaceted and, to some extent, touches almost everyone. As Bettye Caldwell, president of the National Association for the Education of Young Children (NAEYC), states:

> ...we need to work vigorously to help people understand that child care touches the lives of all children to some extent. Rather than a dichotomous service used by some families and not by others, child care is a service that lies along a continuum. All children are reared *primarily* in their own homes by their own families, and virtually all children receive *some* degree of supplemental care from nonfamily members. The difference is more a matter of degree than kind...[4]

Because it is a subject that affects virtually everyone to some degree, day care is frequently the focus of media attention. Articles in newspapers and weekly news magazines highlight the concerns of parents regarding the enormous costs associated with child care, the dilemma of finding quality care for one's children, and the continuing controversy over regulating centers and day care homes and training and keeping adequate and qualified staff. And, of course, recent news reports have brought to light various abuses associated with centers that care for preschool-age children.

Understandably, the majority of these reports focus on the newsworthiness of each story. Few publications have the resources and/or desire to explore, in an in-depth manner, specific issues associated with day care. Such investigation and study is left primarily to the numerous individuals, organizations, and agencies concerned with channeling their energies toward providing quality care for the children of working parents. It is from such resources that the articles included in *Current Issues in Day Care: Readings and Resources* have been drawn. However, the number of articles that are substantive enough to appeal to a professional audience (such as day care personnel), and yet are of broad enough interest to a general audience (largely made up of parents), is limited. The articles in this book have been chosen to reflect the diverse concerns of professionals and parents and, as a result, have been gathered from a wide range of sources.

This book is divided into various sections; "An Overview of Day Care" surveys the current and future needs of families requiring child care and efforts being made to expand and strengthen services. "Day Care Options" looks at specific aspects of day care such as a center-based child care for older children of working parents.

An increasingly popular option for parents is the availability of child care through one's place of employment. Exemplary programs are detailed in the section on "Employer-Sponsored Day Care." While the entire book is of interest to parents, they will be particularly interested in the section on "Parental Concerns." This section offers guidelines for evaluating and selecting appropriate care. Other prominent issues addressed are illness, injuries, and sexual abuse.

The remainder of this book contains resources for parents and day care providers. An annotated bibliography lists current references on various topics related to day care and provides brief synopses of the materials. The appendices contain the results of studies regarding the regulation of day care in the United States and a list of organizations and agencies involved in child care.

REFERENCES

1. U.S. Bureau of the Census, *Statistical Abstract of the United States: 1984* . 104th edition. (Washington, DC: U.S. Government Printing Office, 1983).

2. *America's Children and Their Families: Key Facts* (Washington, DC: Children's Defense Fund, 1982).

3. U.S. Department of Health, Education, and Welfare, *Statistical Highlights from the National Child Care Consumer Study* (Washington, DC: U.S. Department of Health, Education, and Welfare, 1976).

4. Bettye M. Caldwell, "How Can We Educate the American Public About the Child Care Profession?" *Young Children* 38 (3) (March 1983): 11–17.

Contributors

Diane Adams is Assistant Director, Community Coordinated Child Care, Madison, WI. "Family Day Care Registration: Is It Deregulation or More Feasible State Public Policy?" is reprinted from *Young Children* (May 1984, vol. 39, no. 4, pp. 74–78) with permission from the publisher. "National Survey of Family Day Care Regulations: Summary of Findings" (ERIC Document ED 220 207, July 1982) is reprinted with permission from the author.

Susan S. Aronson, M.D. is Clinical Associate Professor of Pediatrics, Hahnemann University, Philadelphia, PA, and Clinical Associate Professor, Community and Preventive Medicine, Medical College of Pennsylvania, Philadelphia, PA. "Injuries in Child Care" is reprinted from *Young Children* (September 1983, vol. 38, no. 5, pp. 19–20) with permission from the author.

Helen Blank is Director of Child Care and Family Support Services for the Children's Defense Fund, Washington, DC. "Initiatives Around the Country" is reprinted with permission from *Child Care Information Exchange* (March 1985, pp. 29–30), P.O. Box 2890, Redmond, WA 98073. "Child Care in the Year 2000" (ERIC Document ED 248 028, paper presented to the Minnesota Early Childhood Roundtable [CEED], May 1984) is reprinted with permission from the author.

Julie Carvalho is an analyst in the Office for Civil Rights, U. S. Department of Health and Human Services, Washington, DC. She has given many presentations on child care and has been honored for her work in the area of civil rights, child care advocacy, and social science research. "Child Care At Conferences: A Family Approach" is reprinted from *Children Today* (May/June 1982, vol. 11, no. 3, pp. 11–15) with permission from the author and publisher.

Brenda Krause Eheart is Director, Developmental Child Care Program, University of Illinois at Urbana-Champaign, Champaign, IL. "Supporting Toddler Play" by Brenda Krause Eheart and Robin Lynn Leavitt is reprinted with permission of the publisher from *Toddler Day Care: A Guide to Responsive Caregiving* by Robin Lynn Leavitt and Brenda Krause Eheart (Lexington, MA: Lexington Books, D. C. Heath and Company, copyright 1985, D. C. Heath and Company).

Rick Graser, a freelance writer based in Washington, DC, is author of "Employer-Sponsored Child Care on the Rise," which appeared in *Appalachia, Journal of the Appalachian Regional Commission,* (November/December 1983, vol. 17, no. 2, pp. 15–21) and is reprinted with permission from the publisher.

Charles Hennon is Assistant Professor and an extension specialist, Family Resources and Consumer Sciences, University of Wisconsin–Madison, WI. "Industry-Related Day Care: Trends and Options" by Marce Verzaro-O'Brien, Denise LeBlanc, and Charles Hennon is reprinted from *Young Children* (January 1982, vol. 37, no. 2, pp. 4–10) with permission from the publisher.

Sheila B. Kamerman is Professor of Social Policy and Planning, Columbia University School of Social Work, New York, NY, and Codirector, Cross-National Studies Research Program. She is the author of numerous books, monographs, and articles and has served as consultant to federal, state, and local agencies, organizations and foundations concerned, in part, with child welfare and child care. "Child-Care Services: A National Picture" is reprinted from *Monthly Labor Review* (December 1983, vol. 106, no. 12, pp. 35–39) with permission from the author and the Bureau of Labor Statistics of the U. S. Department of Labor.

Earline D. Kendall is Chair, Department of Education, Belmont College, Nashville, TN. "Child Care and Disease: What Is the Link" is reprinted from *Young Children* (July 1983, vol. 38, no. 5, pp. 68–77) with permission from the National Association for the Education of Young Children. "Day Care Licensing: The Eroding Regulations" by Earline D. Kendall and Lewis H. Walker is reprinted from *Child Care Quarterly* (Winter 1984, vol. 13, no. 4, pp. 278–90) with permission from the publisher.

Judith P. LaVorgna is Executive Director, Cenvill Family Centers, Inc., Coconut Creek, FL. She has been a kindergarten and early childhood teacher as well as director of various day care facilities and a university instructor. She is active in consulting and has many publications to her credit. "Schools in the Workplace" is reprinted from *Phi Delta*

Kappan (October 1982, vol. 64, no. 2, pp. 128–29) with permission from the author and the publisher.

Robin Lynn Leavitt is Specialist, Early Childhood Education, and Director, Day Care Home Project, University of Illinois at Urbana-Champaign, Champaign, IL. "Supporting Toddler Play" by Brenda Krause Eheart and Robin Lynn Leavitt is reprinted with permission of the publisher from *Toddler Day Care: A Guide to Responsive Caregiving* by Robin Lynn Leavitt and Brenda Krause Eheart (Lexington, MA: Lexington Books, D. C. Heath and Company, copyright 1985, D. C. Heath and Company).

Denise LeBlanc is Lecturer, Human Development and Family Living, University of Wisconsin, Stout–Menomonie, WI. "Industry-Related Day Care: Trends and Options" by Marce Verzaro-O'Brien, Denise LeBlanc, and Charles Hennon is reprinted from *Young Children* (January 1982, vol. 37, no. 2, pp. 4–10) with permission from the publisher.

Marion R. McNairy is Assistant Professor of Early Childhood Education, Department of Curriculum and Instruction, School of Education, Indiana University, Bloomington, IN. "School-Age Child Care: Program and Policy Issues" is reprinted from *Educational Horizons* (Winter 1984, vol. 62, no. 2, pp. 64–67) with permission from the author and Pi Lamda Theta.

Peggy Lewis Nieting is Early School and Child Care Director, Coastal Academy, Myrtle Beach, SC. "School-Age Child Care: In Support of Development and Learning" is reprinted from *Childhood Education* (September/October 1983, vol. 60, no. 1, pp. 6–11). Reprinted by permission of Peggy Lewis Nieting and the Association for Childhood Education International, 11141 Georgia Avenue, Suite 200, Wheaton, MD. Copyright ©1983 by the Association.

Aimee Nover is Codirector, Clara Barton Center for Children, Cabin John, MD. "Day Care and Community: The Necessary Partnership" by Aimee Nover and Ann Segal is reprinted from *Children Today* (May/June 1978, vol. 7, no. 3, pp. 2–6) with permission from the authors and the publisher.

Peggy Patten has been a teacher of preschool and kindergarten-aged children for 9 years and has served on the faculty of the University of Illinois at Urbana-Champaign Child Development Laboratory. "How to Choose the Best Day-Care Program for Your Child" is reprinted from *PTA Today* (April 1984, vol. 9, no. 6, pp. 4–6) with permission from the National PTA, Chicago, IL.

J. Frank Popplewell is Systems Analyst, Amherst H. Wiler Foundation, St. Paul, MN. He was formerly Research Assistant for the Child Care Coun-

cil of Ramsey County. "Including Parents in Evaluating Family Day Care Homes" by Mary Winget, W. Gary Winget, and J. Frank Popplewell is reprinted from *Child Welfare* (April 1982, vol. 61, no. 4, pp. 195–205) with permission from the Child Welfare League of America, Inc.

Carolyn Reece is Editor, *Children Today,* Washington, DC. "Bringing Children To Work: A Hospital Day Care Center" is reprinted from *Children Today* (July/August 1982, vol. 11, no. 4, pp. 16–19, 21) with permission from the author and the publisher.

Ann Segal is Codirector, Clara Barton Center for Children, Cabin John, MD. "Day Care and Community: The Necessary Partnership" by Aimee Nover and Ann Segal is reprinted from *Children Today* (May/June 1978, vol. 7, no. 3, pp. 2–6) with permission from the authors and the publisher.

"The Sexual Abuse Issue: How Can Child Care Providers Respond?" is reprinted from *Child Care Information Exchange* (August 1984, pp. 20–24) with permission from Child Care Information Exchange, P. O. Box 2890, Redmond, WA 98073. This article was compiled by Roger Neugebauer, publisher of *Child Care Information Exchange* and *Beginnings,* and his staff.

Candace E. Trunzo is a staff writer with *Money* magazine, New York, NY. "The ABC's of Selecting a Day-Care Center" is reprinted from *Money* (September 1984, vol. 13, no. 9, pp. 173–74, 176, 178, 180) by special permission: ©1984, Time Inc.

Marce Verzaro-O'Brien is Assistant Professor of Early Childhood Education, State University of New York College at Buffalo. "Industry-Related Day Care: Trends and Options" by Marce Verzaro-O'Brien, Denise LeBlanc, and Charles Hennon is reprinted from *Young Children* (January 1982, vol. 37, no. 2, pp. 4–10) with permission from the publisher.

Lewis H. Walker is a research assistant with the Betty Phillips Center for Parenthood Education at the George Peabody College for Teachers of Vanderbilt University, Nashville, TN. "Day Care Licensing: The Eroding Regulations" by Earline D. Kendall and Lewis H. Walker is reprinted from *Child Care Quarterly* (Winter 1984, vol. 13, no. 4, pp. 278–90) with permission from the publisher.

Mary Winget is a freelance writer based in New Haven, CT. "Including Parents in Evaluating Family Day Care Homes" by Mary Winget, W. Gary Winget, and J. Frank Popplewell is reprinted from *Child Welfare* (April 1982, vol. 61, no. 4, pp. 195–205) with permission from the Child Welfare League of America, Inc.

W. Gary Winget is Executive Director, Child Care Council of Ramsey County, St. Paul, MN.

"Including Parents in Evaluating Family Day Care Homes" by Mary Winget, W. Gary Winget, and J. Frank Popplewell is reprinted from *Child Welfare* (April 1982, vol. 61, no. 4, pp. 195–205) with permission from the Child Welfare League of America, Inc.

Section I:
An Overview of Day Care

Introduction

This first section is designed to be introductory in nature. The articles chosen for inclusion provide an overview of the types of child care services used by parents and also point out some of the current and future concerns such as cost, funding, regulations, and quality of care. Responses to the need for child care from federal and state governments, as well as from private sectors, are discussed.

The first article is by Sheila B. Kamerman, the author of several works relating to day care and issues of concern to women. "Child-Care Services: A National Picture" addresses child care alternatives being considered by working parents in America, the quality of the care in such arrangements, and some of the current trends and issues in the child care field. She emphasizes that although there is a lack of accurate data concerning needed services, particularly for infants and toddlers, the need for affordable, accessible, and quality child care will not only continue to be a pressing need but will undoubtedly increase in the future.

Current and future needs for such services are described by Helen Blank, director of Child Care and Family Services for the Children's Defense Fund. "Initiatives Around the Country" reports on both national and state efforts toward funding and regulating child care. She emphasizes some of the problems associated with new federal guidelines tied to monies for training child care providers. Several states are highlighted for their efforts toward seeking funding for child care and for upgrading licensing standards. Issues that all state legislators may eventually have to deal with are considered here.

The final article in this section, also by Helen Blank, provides a glimpse into the future. "Child Care in the Year 2000" attempts to predict how present-day inadequacies in the area of day care will affect future generations. She looks at the population needing such services in the year 2000 and speculates on how these needs will be met. She also discusses the probable competition for resources from such groups as the elderly, which will make up a proportionately larger part of the population by the end of this century.

Child-care services: a national picture

As more mothers hold jobs, the demand for child-care services continues to grow—especially for infant and toddler care—and is exacerbated by brief maternity leaves

SHEILA B. KAMERMAN

In 1983, for the first time, half of all mothers with children under age 6 were in the labor force.[1] Out of a cohort of 19.0 million children under age 6, 47 percent had working mothers. In the near future, the *majority* of preschoolers will very likely have working mothers, as most school-age children already do. How preschool children are cared for while their mothers work is something that relatively little is known about, although what is known suggests a quite complicated picture.

What is the picture today of child-care services for preschool aged children? To help the reader visualize the picture, four questions are addressed:

• Where are the children of working parents being cared for?
• What is known about the kinds of child-care services and arrangements that now exist?
• What is known about the quality of care now provided and what is happening to it?
• What are the current trends, developments, and emerging issues in the child-care services field?

For the purposes of this article, child-care services will include: family day care and center care, public and private nursery school and prekindergartens, Head Start centers, all-day care, part-day care, and after-school care. (Non-monetized care by relatives and brief, occasional babysitting are not included.) The discussion is about relatively regular care or attendance: a specific number of hours per day and regular days per week of provision—in families and group arrangements—under both educational and social welfare auspices.

Types and amount of available child care

Unfortunately, in addition to the child-care picture not being very clear, it is not very complete. National data are not collected in any systematic fashion on: children in out-of-home care during the day; child-care arrangements used while parents work; or child-care service programs. To study what exists and who uses which type of care, one must piece together different, sometimes not fully comparable data, collected by different sources at different times.

In providing an overview of child-care services for preschool aged children, the types of services can be distinguished by the following:

• The age of the child:
—infant and toddler care (0 to 2-year-olds)
—preschooler care (3- to 5-year-olds)

• The locus of care:
—in own home
—in a relative's home
—in a nonrelative's home
—in a group facility (center or school)

• The auspice of care:
—education (nursery school, prekindergarten, kindergarten)
—social welfare (day-care center)

• The source of funds:
—direct and indirect public subsidy (for example, public grants of monies to a provider or a tax benefit such as the child-care tax credit)
—private subsidy
—employer subsidy; parent fees

Preschoolers. Although there are no precise figures concerning the numbers of children in out-of-home care, by age of child and type of care, the most complete data to date are those on preschool children aged 3 to 5. However, even here estimates must be used.

The most recent national survey of day-care centers was completed by Abt Associates in 1977;[2] the numbers are known to have grown substantially since then. Moreover, these data do not include programs under educational auspices: nursery schools, prekindergartens, and kindergartens. These are the largest single type of child-care services for children of this age and the most rapidly growing component among child-care services for this age group.

The most currently published consumer data on 3- and 4-year-old children of working mothers are from a 1977 Current Population Survey (CPS) conducted by the Bureau of the Census.[3] Only data on children *under age 5* and on the *youngest* child in the family were included. However, because the survey was carried out in June, when many schools are closed, children in group care programs are significantly underreported. For example, fewer than 21 percent of children of this age with mothers who worked full time in 1977 were reported as enrolled in group care, as contrasted with 31 percent of *all* children this age in 1976, according to Census Bureau school enrollment data,[4] and 37 percent in 1980, as cited by the National Center for Educational Statistics.[5] (See tables 1 and 2.) Furthermore, the proportion of youngsters enrolled in preschool programs was significantly higher when their mothers worked (44 percent). Moreover, these data do not report multiple modes of care: the "packages" of child-care arrangements which

Table 1. Population of preschoolers, preprimary school enrollment, and labor force status of mother by child's age, 1980

Child's age (in years)	Total (in millions)	Enrollment Numbers (in millions)	Enrollment Percent of total	Percent with mothers in labor force
3 to 5	9.3	4.9[1]	53[1]	57
5	3.1	2.6	84[2]	85
3 to 4	6.2	2.3	37	43
4	3.1	1.4	46	52
3	3.1	.9	29	34

[1]Preprimary programs only. An additional number are enrolled in primary school (about 3 percent of cohort).
[2]An additional 9 percent are enrolled in primary school.
NOTE: Data are for 50 States and District of Columbia.
SOURCE: National Center for Education Statistics, *Preprimary Enrollment 1980* (Washington, D.C., U.S. Department of Education, 1982).

are most frequently used by working mothers.[6] Such "packages" include some combination of a preschool program, family day care, and relative care; they may involve four or more different care givers during an average week. More extensive child-care data were collected in the 1982 Census Bureau's national fertility survey, but these data had not yet been published when this article was prepared.

Using 1979 school enrollment data[7] and data from the 1977 Abt supply study of day-care enrollment, it is found that almost two-thirds of *all* 3- to 5-year-olds and more than 70 percent of those with working mothers are in some form of group child-care program. These numbers are made up of the following: ninety-three percent of all 5-year-olds were in nursery school, kindergarten, or first grade in 1979. Thirty-five percent of all 3- to 4-year-olds were in nursery school or prekindergarten. A growing number of these preschool programs are full day; the proportion of 3- to 5-year-olds in a full-day program doubled during the 1970's, from 17 percent in 1970, to 34 percent in 1980. By 1980, 37 percent

of 3- to 4-year-olds were in preprimary programs. Although kindergarten enrollment for 5-year-olds is about the same whether or not mothers work (almost all 5-year-olds are in preschool or primary school), enrollment rates for 3- to 4-year-olds are significantly higher when mothers are in the labor force (44 percent, compared with 31 percent in 1980). All-day enrollment is, of course, far higher for children with full-time working mothers. Although these programs may be valued for their educational content, they are often used because they fulfill a needed child-care function.

Kindergarten enrollment increased by almost one-third between 1967 and 1980 (from 65 to 85 percent). However, the increase in nursery school enrollment has been even more dramatic, doubling in numbers during the 1970's and more than doubling as a proportion of 3- to 4-year-olds enrolled (from 16 percent in 1969 to 37 percent in 1980).

Moreover, not only are children of working mothers more likely to be enrolled in preschool programs, but the enrollment rates are even higher when mothers have larger incomes and more education. Fifty-three percent of 3- to 4-year-old children in families with median or higher incomes attended a preschool program in 1982, as contrasted with only 29 percent of those in lower income families. As noted, enrollment rates increase as mothers' education levels rise, and increase still more when those mothers are employed. Only for children whose mothers are college graduates is there no difference between those with working and those with nonworking mothers. For example, about half of such 3-year-olds and 72 percent of such 4-year-olds were in a preschool program in 1982.[8]

Given these data, one could argue that not only is there growing use of preschool as a child-care service for the 3-, 4-, and 5-year-olds with working mothers, but there is especially high use by affluent, educated, working families.

Table 2. Preprimary school enrollment by child's age and labor force status of mother, 1980

[Numbers in thousands]

Labor force status of mother	Total Enrolled	Total Enrolled all day	3-year-olds Enrolled	3-year-olds Enrolled all day	4-year-olds Enrolled	4-year-olds Enrolled all day	5-year-olds Enrolled	5-year-olds Enrolled all day
All children, 3 to 5 years	4,878	1,551	857	321	1,423	467	2,598	763
With mother in labor force	2,480	1,002	497	260	755	332	1,229	413
Employed full time	1,445	713	292	198	457	260	696	255
Employed part time	811	196	163	42	245	44	402	111
Unemployed	225	94	41	20	53	28	131	46
With mother not in labor force	2,266	491	339	50	628	117	1,299	325
Keeping house	2,105	439	309	37	582	102	1,214	300
Other	85	15	15	3	23	3	47	9
No mother present	131	57	21	13	39	19	70	26
	Enrolled as percent of age group							
All children, 3 to 5 years	52.5	16.7	27.3	10.2	46.3	15.2	84.7	24.9
With mother in labor force	57.1	23.1	34.4	18.0	51.9	22.8	85.2	28.6
Employed full time	57.4	23.3	35.4	24.0	52.5	29.9	84.6	31.0
Employed part time	59.6	14.4	37.2	9.6	53.7	9.6	86.5	23.9
Unemployed	48.5	20.3	22.8	11.1	41.1	21.7	85.1	29.9
With mother not in labor force	48.9	10.6	21.5	3.2	41.5	7.7	84.5	21.1
Keeping house	48.5	10.1	20.9	2.5	40.2	7.2	83.9	20.7
In school	63.0	29.5	37.2	([1])	56.1	([1])	95.1	([1])
Other	51.1	9.0	26.4	([1])	38.3	([1])	95.9	([1])
No mother present	42.2	12.5	17.8	10.8	38.6	18.8	77.8	28.9

[1]Base too small for presentation of percentage.
NOTE: Data are for 50 States and District of Columbia. Details may not add to totals because of rounding.
SOURCE: National Center for Education Statistics, *Preprimary Enrollment, 1980* (Washington, D.C., U.S. Department of Education, 1982.

Because most of these programs are private and relatively expensive, such high use by the more affluent raises serious questions about the consequences for those children in lower income families (below median income) without access to such programs, whether or not their mothers work.

According to the Abt survey, in addition to those children in preschool programs, about 10 percent of the cohort (900,000) were in day-care centers (most were 3- or 4-year-olds). Thus, there seems to be a total of 54 percent of the 3- and 4-year-olds with working mothers in some kind of group care for some part of the day. This figure is likely to be higher because nearly a half million children are estimated to have been enrolled in Title XX funded centers in 1981, a significant increase over the 1977 figures.[9] (And 10 States were not included in the 1981 figure because they did not provide data.) Sixty-five percent of these children were 3- to 5-year-olds (and more than half were age 3 or 4); and almost all had working parents (these figures may have decreased in the past year). Also, Head Start serves nearly 400,000 children, largely 3- and 4-year-olds.

Federally funded (Title XX) centers have increased in numbers, too: there were an estimated 11,342 in 1981, a significant jump from the 8,100 identified in the Abt survey.[10] Some of these centers may have closed in the past year as a consequence of cutbacks in funding, but no specific data on closings are available as of this writing. Head Start programs have also expanded since 1977 and about one-fifth are full-day programs. More than 40 percent of the day-care centers in the Abt survey were proprietary or for-profit establishments. Both the numbers and the proportion of proprietary child-care services have grown significantly since then. Because most of the large (multicenter) for-profit child-care service companies did not receive Title XX money in 1981, these numbers are additive rather than overlapping.

In addition, about 42 percent of 3- to 4-year-olds whose mothers worked full time in 1977 (and 25 percent of those whose mothers worked part time) were cared for in someone else's home, usually in a nonrelative's home (family day care).[11] There is a significant, if unknown, overlap between the children in preschool programs and those cared for in a home, be it by a relative or nonrelative, part of the child-care "packaging" mentioned above, and particularly important for children whose mothers work longer than the preschool or school hours. About 100,000 children were in federally funded family day-care homes in 1981.[12] By far, most children in family day care (about 90 percent of the more than 6 million children estimated to be in family day care for 10 hours or more per week in 1975) were in informal, unregulated care.[13] About 6 percent were in licensed care, including 2 percent in care provided in a home but under the sponsorship of an umbrella agency. However, most of these children were under age 3.

Infants and toddlers. As difficult as it is to estimate coverage and type of care provided for preschoolers, the data on infant and toddler care are far less adequate. A planned national survey of infant care, to be carried out by Abt, was cancelled. The much-cited National Consumer Day Care Study was poorly designed and inadequately analyzed. According to the 1977 Current Population Survey, the primary care arrangement for children under age 3 was family day care, usually in the home of a nonrelative.

Estimating from the CPS data, more than one-third of the children with working mothers were in either family day care or group care in 1977. More specifically, about one-third of those under age 3 with full-time working mothers and 17 percent of those with part-time working mothers were in family day care; and more than 9 percent of those with full-time working mothers and 5.5 percent of those whose mothers worked part time were in group care. Infant and toddler care has been growing rapidly since the mid-1970's; thus, the coverage data are undoubtedly higher today.

The following rounds out this picture of how children are cared for while parents (especially mothers) are in the labor force:

- A small proportion of babies with working mothers are cared for, albeit briefly, by mothers on maternity leave. Fewer than 40 percent of working mothers are entitled to some paid leave at the time of childbirth, usually for about 6 to 8 weeks, and a somewhat larger group may remain home on an unpaid but job-protected leave for 3 or 4 months.[14]

- Some parents, especially those with preschool aged children, work different shifts in order to manage child care. Although this method of care has received very little attention thus far, researchers using three different data sets (the Current Population Survey, the Panel Study of Income Dynamics, and the Quality of Employment Survey) have found that this may be a more significant pattern of work by parents with young children than suspected.[15]

- A very few employers, largely hospitals, provide onsite child-care services (about 230 hospitals; about 50 employers), and a few others subsidize payment of care.[16]

Child-care quality: programming and standards

More than half of all nursery schools are private, 66 percent. Eighty-eight percent of the kindergartens are public. There are limited national data available on these programs. On the other hand, a much more extensive picture exists regarding the more than 11,000 federally funded day-care centers that existed in the fall of 1981. This type of center is discussed here.

In early 1980, the Department of Health and Human Services issued proposed day-care regulations concerning group size, staff-to-child ratios, training qualifications for care givers, nutrition, health care, parent participation, and social services, to become effective in October. In the meantime, the Congress, in its Omnibus Budget Reconciliation Act of 1980, delayed the effective date of these proposed regulations. Before the proposals could become effective, the Social Services Block Grant Act was enacted. Among other things, this Act amended Federal requirements and standards regarding Title XX day-care centers. This meant that State and local standards, where they existed, were in effect. (Such standards are likely to be below those set by the Federal Government.)

The Omnibus Budget Reconciliation Act mandated the Department of Health and Human Services to "assist each State in conducting a systematic assessment of current practices in Title XX funded day-care programs and provide a summary report of the assessment to Congress by June 1, 1981."[17] According to the report, provider practices were in compliance with or surpassed the proposed Federal standards. More specifically:

- Despite the fact that 24 of the 47 States reporting have no group size requirements, all stated their centers had groups smaller than those set in the proposed regulations for all but the under-2-year-olds.
- Staff-to-child ratios were significantly higher than proposed for children aged 3 and older; however, they were significantly lower for those under 3.
- Although only half the States required the centers to provide training, nearly all provided such training and three-quarters of centers' care givers and one-half of family day-care mothers had gone through such a training program within the past year.
- Seventy-five percent of the centers (and half of the homes) provided the Department of Agriculture's recommended child-care food program.
- Seventy percent of the States assured children in care funded by Title XX the needed health services and 75 percent assured them needed social services.

Federal funding under Title XX has been significantly cut since 1981. Day care was one of the three highest funded Title XX services, representing 18 percent of all Title XX expenditures nationwide. Funding for the child nutrition program, a component of public support of day care, has also been reduced. Few programs have actually closed thus far, but this may occur in the future. Given the large cutbacks in Federal grants to States, most States are under growing financial pressure in this area. These States will view themselves as fortunate if they can maintain the quantity of care; they are unlikely to enforce standards, even if standards exist.

A question emerges regarding whether the extent of compliance that existed in 1981 was not related to the expectations of Federal standards and enforcement. From now on, the States will have primary responsibility for setting and enforcing standards concerning the health, safety, and developmental needs of children in care. Whether providers will continue to maintain these standards and whether States will monitor what providers do remains to be seen. Thus, day-care regulation joins preprimary school generally as an arena in which the protection of children will depend completely on the State.

Towards the future

The only significant Federal development is the expansion of the child-care tax credit in 1982 and, subsequently, making it available even to those who do not itemize deductions. However, unless the credit is increased, and made refundable, it will have no—or very little—value to low- and moderate-income families.

The Dependent Care Assistance plan and the salary reduction plan for certain private insurance benefits may open the way for some expansion in employer-sponsored child-care services.[18] However, little has occurred as yet.

The major development in the field in recent years has been child-care information and referral services. These have burgeoned, especially in California, where they are publicly funded; this is an area in which more employers are considering involvement as well. Finally, concern with the quality of education is leading some States and localities to reexamine their preprimary programs. Some are now initiating full-day kindergartens; others are establishing prekindergarten programs; and still others are considering both.

The demand for child-care services continues to grow, and most parents of preschoolers want an educational program. Most such programs are private, particularly those below kindergarten level. Unfortunately, good programs are very often expensive. Moreover, there is still a scarcity of full-day programs, so many parents are "packaging" a group program with one or more other types of care, with consequences not yet known. The cutbacks in funding group programs are especially significant in their impact on services for low- and middle-income children. Many of these children who were in publicly subsidized preschool programs are being transferred into informal and unregulated family day care as subsidies are cut back and programs close or parents lose their eligibility for a subsidy; the children must adapt to a new care giver, and often to the loss of friends.

The biggest current demand for child-care services is for infants and toddlers, because it is among their mothers that the increase in labor force participation has been greatest, and the scarcity of services most severe. Paid maternity (disability) leaves are available only to a minority of working women and are usually brief. There is an urgent need to expand and improve maternity-related benefits provided at the workplace.[19] Data concerning how babies and toddlers are being cared for and what types of care exist are largely inadequate. Most of these children are in informal family day-care arrangements but, here again, little is known about these services.

Although the current child-care picture is hardly complete, all that is known suggests the likelihood of continuing demand. Accessibility, affordability, and quantity will remain central issues but questions regarding *quality* will increasingly come to the forefront. □

————*FOOTNOTES*————

ACKNOWLEDGMENT: This article is based on work done as a part of a national study of child-care services sponsored by the Carnegie Corporation.

[1] Elizabeth Waldman, "Labor force statistics from a family perspective," *Monthly Labor Review*, December 1983, pp. 14–18.

[2] U.S. Department of Health and Human Services, Administration for Children, Youth, and Families, in collaboration with Abt Associates, Inc. (Cambridge, Mass.), *National Day Care Study* (Washington, U.S. Government Printing Office, 1979), and *National Day Care Home Study* (Washington, U.S. Government Printing Office, 1980).

[3] *Trends in Child Care Arrangements of Working Mothers, Current Population Reports*, Series P–23, No. 117 (Bureau of the Census, 1982).

[4] *Nursery School and Kindergarten Enrollment of Children and Labor Force Status of Their Mothers, October 1967 to October 1976, Current Population Reports*, Series P–20, No. 318 (Bureau of the Census, 1978).

[5] *Preprimary Enrollment 1980* (U.S. Department of Education, National Center for Educational Statistics, 1982).

[6] Mary Jo Bane, Laura Lein, Lydia O'Donnell, C. Ann Stueve, and Barbara Wells, "Child care arrangements of working parents," *Monthly Labor Review*, October 1979, pp. 50–56; and Sheila B. Kamerman, *Parenting In An Unresponsive Society: Managing Work and Family Life* (New York, The Free Press, 1980).

[7] *School Enrollment—Social and Economic Characteristics of Students: October 1979, Current Population Reports*, Series P–20, No. 360 (Bureau of the Census, 1981); and *National Day Care Study*.

[8] National Center for Education Statistics, unpublished data.

[9] *Report to Congress, Summary Report of the Assessment of Current State Practices in Title XX Funded Day Care Programs* (U.S. Department of Health and Human Services, Administration for Children, Youth, and Families, 1982).

[10] Ibid.

[11] *Trends in Child Care Arrangements*.

[12] *Report to Congress*.

[13] UNCO, Inc., *National Child Care Consumer Study: 1975* (U.S. Department of Health, Education, and Welfare, 1977).

[14] Sheila B. Kamerman, Alfred F. Kahn, and Paul W. Kingston, *Maternity Policies and Working Women* (New York, Columbia University Press, 1983).

[15] Steven L. Nock and Paul W. Kingston, "The Family Workday," *Journal of Marriage and the Family*, forthcoming; Harriet B. Presser, "Working Women and Child Care," in P.W. Berman and E.R. Ramey, eds., *Women: A Developmental Perspective* (Washington, U.S. Government Printing Office, 1982); and Graham L. Staines and Joseph H. Pleck, "Work Schedules' Impact on the Family," Research Monograph, 1982, processed.

[16] Sandra L. Burud, Raymond C. Collins, Patricia Divine-Hawkins, "Employer-Supported Child Care: Everybody Benefits," *Children Today*, May–June 1983, pp. 2–7.

[17] See *Report to Congress*. The data provided in this report are baseline data for future assessments of the quality of Title XX funded day care once these programs are no longer subject to Federal regulations.

[18] For a description of these benefits, see Sheila B. Kamerman, *Meeting Family Needs: the Corporate Response* (White Plains, N.Y., Work in America, forthcoming).

[19] Kamerman, Kahn, and Kingston, *Maternity Policies*.

Initiatives Around the Country

by Helen Blank

It is expected that the child care reports issued by the Select Committee for Children, Youth, and Families will set the stage for the introduction of a series of bills which could provide increased federal support for child care. However, given the fact that *the deficit is significantly larger* than the Reagan Administration expected, advocates seeking new monies for child care face an unusual challenge. The Administration has proposed significant cuts in human services programs; but given a *more liberal* Senate and less Republican gains than predicted in the House, it is not certain that Congress will embrace the Reagan budget numbers. While many legislators are eager to sponsor child care bills, most are seeking only modest amounts to address the less than modest need for new resources in child care.

Funding for Child Care Block Grant

One of the first agenda items will be an attempt to seek funding in a supplemental appropriations bill for the school-age and resource and referral block grant which was included in S 2565, a bill reauthorizing the Head Start program. The FY 1985 appropriations bill for labor and human services program did not include funding for the new child care block grant.

Training Monies Requirements

PL 98-473, the FY 1985 continuing resolution, appropriates $25 million in additional Title XX funds for one year to be used for training child care providers, operators, staffs, state licensing enforcement officials, and parents. States which accept the training monies must, by October 1, 1985, establish procedures by state law or regulations to provide for employment history and background checks as well as a state law which requires a criminal record check for all existing and prospective operators, staff, and employees of all child care programs having *primary custody of a child for at least 20 hours a week* and all juvenile detention, correction, and treatment facilities. If states take the funds and do not implement the requirements, they will in FY 1986 or 1987 have an amount equal to half of their training funds subtracted from their Title XX social services block grant allotment.

The law is very vague, providing little direction to states. Key issues that must be considered if a state is considering implementing procedures for criminal record checks include:

● Which state agencies or combination of agencies (i.e. licensing, justice) will be responsible for the process?

● Who will retain the information sent from the FBI?

● How will employers be notified of employees' convictions?

● What crimes will constitute a valid reason for denying employment?

● Who pays for the background checks which may cost between $12 and $20? Will it be states, providers, prospective employees?

● How will records be updated for current employees?

● What appeal rights are guaranteed to employees and prospective employees?

● How are substitute caregivers and volunteers treated under the law?

● Should programs like nursery schools which serve children less than 20 hours a week be covered by the law?

● Will employers also be required to check each state's central child abuse registry?

● What issues should be considered if child abuse registries are used?

Minnesota: Child Care Works

Three groups in Minnesota (Greater Minneapolis Day Care, Rochester's Child Care Resource and Referral, and Resources for Child Caring) have joined together with a broad coalition of church, women's, child care, and government groups in an effort called **Child Care Works**. Their major agenda items include:

● an increase of $40 million in the state's sliding fee child care program;

● start-up funds for resource and referral programs;

● increased funds and authority for child care licensing.

New York: Initiatives

New York's child care community did not win passage of the Working Parents' Act which would have provided $10 million targeted to child care. They are hopeful that this year their efforts will be successful. They did manage to pass several smaller initiatives including $300,000 for school-age programs and $1.5 million from higher education funds to promote child care services of the State University of New York and the City University of New York. In 1985 they will seek $12 million to provide a funding stream for subsidy of child care services for low and modest income children.

In addition, the New York State Child Care Coordinating Council will support legislation favorable to funding for child care resource and referral services provided by non-profit community agencies. It will also highlight the importance of resource and referral agencies in family child care support, ask that job training programs include funds for child care, support additional funds to start school-age programs. Finally, the Council will support legislation that would enable transportation via public school buses for school-age children to after-school programs to be considered an ordinary contingent.

California: Funds for School-Age Child Care

California mobilized its very organized child care community this fall in a massive effort to convince their governor to sign a bill providing $35 million for FY 1984 and 1985 and $60 million annually thereafter for school-age programs. Although he vetoed the bill, claiming that the issue required further study, advocates will be back seeking even more funds for school-age child care.

Illinois: Consumer Education Materials

Illinois expects to adopt child care licensing requirements which will require child care providers to distribute to parents consumer education materials concerning licensing standards, selecting child care, communicable disease, and prevention and reporting of child abuse. Parents will have to sign a statement indicating that they have received this information.

Connecticut: Funds for New Facilities

Connecticut passed two bills this summer to help provide funds to support new child care facilities:

● $350,000 in grants to state agencies and municipalities to establish child care facilities primarily for their employees.

● $250,000 in low-interest loans to non-profit organizations such as schools and hospitals to establish child care facilities primarily for their employees. A revolving loan fund would be administered by the Department of Economic Development; loans would be repaid within five years, and the cost would not exceed one percent of bonding costs.

Another act established a Day Care Study Commission to study the regulatory function of child care and the most cost-effective use of public funds for regulation.

Georgia: Advocacy Network

A new advocacy network is being formed in the Atlanta metropolitan area which could mean good news for child care. Ninety-six organizations are already dues-paying members of the group which plans to include economic justice as a major agenda item. Nancy Travis of Save the Children's southern states office is on the Steering Committee and will help to insure that child care issues are a key focus.

Child Care in the Year 2000

by Helen Blank

Will the traditional American value system which has thus far seen child care as a parental responsibility shift enough to allow for the building of a child care system that is responsive to the rapidly changing demographics? Will we ever come close to accepting the principles underlying the development of Sweden's comprehensive child care system which includes:

- The right of both men and women to work.

- The equality of sexes.

- The possibility of both parents to devote time to their children.

Even if our values take a turn in a new direction and every child and family is guaranteed the right to a supportive and safe child care experience in the year 2000, there is another serious issue intimately linked to early childhood that we as a society will face as a nation in the year 2000. The parents of many of our pre-school children will bear the scars of the child care policies of the 1980's which have resulted in relatively bleak early childhood experiences for a large percentage of this population entering parenting age in the year 2000.

A large segment of the new parents will have been affected by the lack of supportive child care policies. Currently more than one-fifth of all children live in households with incomes below the poverty level, while 40.7 percent of all black families with children live below the poverty level.

It is important to remember that these same parents and their own parents suffered the effects of cutbacks in health services, loss of income supports, and the ultimate stress that results from living at a bare minimum level of subsistence.

In child care specifically the results of 1981 cuts are grim. Thirty-three states served less children in 1983 than 1981. What does this mean to the quality of the early lives of the children who lost care? West Virginia is not an atypical state—739 families lost care. A survey revealed that at least 391 children had been shifted from familiar child care arrangements, forced to leave their familiar caregivers and friends, while 79 children were

caring for themselves. In New York State between 8400 and 12,000 children lost child care. One-sixth of these children are reported to be regularly caring for themselves.

Many of the parents in the year 2000 will be the 600,000 babies who were born to adolescent mothers in 1984. Few will have been fortunate enough to be cared for in child care settings in high schools enabling their mothers to finish their education.

Many parents will have had mothers who remained dependent on AFDC because of the limited child care supports available to mothers in school or training programs.

These parents will all have had extremely different pre-school experiences from the 53 percent of children from middle and upper-income families who were enrolled in pre-school in 1984. Their own parents were unlikely to take much advantage of the dependent care tax credit, a $2 billion program which is most useful to families with the income to pay for child care in the first place. Many of them who grew up in the one-fifth of all families in 1984 headed by single parents, most of them raised by their mothers, are unlikely to earn more than $10,000 a year.

Their mothers were also the least likely beneficiaries of private sector child benefits. In fact, their parents may have worked at a company who could not use their on-site center because it did not offer a sliding scale, so some may have had companies which provided assistance in helping them find child care but were indifferent to the fact that the cost of the care was beyond the lower-income employee's reach. Most of their parents were not able to take advantage of salary reduction plans due to their limited tax liabilities.

We definitely will have a new generation needing child care in the year 2000. Because of the baby boom, there is a large group of young women currently in the child bearing ages who will raise potential mothers. Immigration will also contribute to the growth in the number of children and the need for child care will be heightened by the continued increase in children living in single parent households. By the year 2000 there will be a 15.6 percent increase in the number of children under six. There will be a sizeable increase in the number of these children living in poverty. If the poverty rate among children under six equals the corresponding rates in 1981, the number of very young children living in poverty will increase by nearly 2 million between 1980 and 1990, an amount for a poverty rate of 25 percent of all children under six.

Clearly, there will be patchwork, some changes in our current child care system.

- Eighty percent of two parent-families will have both spouses employed.
- Seventy-five percent of all mothers will be working.

The use of informal child care arrangements should decline in the year 2000.

- Family day care providers are often women with young children. The recent cohorts of young women are obtaining labor force experience earlier. Such young women will be more likely to continue to work outside the home even after having children.
- The continued increase in female headed households will affect the demand for center based care as they are more likely to use centers.

The continued decline in family size will also result in smaller families better able to afford more formal care in homes or centers.

- Increased mobility will enable fewer families to be able to use relatives for child care.
- Fewer siblings and fewer teen-agers will limit sibling care. Between 1981 and 1995, the number of teen-agers in the population should drop from 27.6 million to 24.4 million.

Before we can speak to the child care system that will be in place in the 1990's, it is important to consider other relevant demographics that could have considerable effect on the resources necessary to build this system. By the year 2000, our elderly population will have increased considerably. The population over 80 is the fastest growing segment of the population. Between 1980 and 1990 alone the total elderly population is expected to grow by 6.3 million with the old-elderly accounting for approximately 2.3 million of the increase. As the share of women, the very old and persons living alone increases, the number of poor elderly will also increase. If the population age 80 and above that is poor remained relatively stable at about 20 percent, there will be 1.5 million versus 1 million in 1983 who are poor in 1990.

How will this affect child care? These are three ramifications:

- A basic competition for dependent care resources. Currently one in 10 million women between 45 and 65 has responsibility for an elder relative. In 1975, almost 1 million women aged 44 to 58 claimed that the health of a family member limits their work. One out of eight retired women said they were retired because they were needed at home. As more women work, more will want to stay in the labor force and seek outside care for their dependents. The increased elderly will also affect the medicare budget.
- A competition for the agenda of women's organizations, many of whom have an aging membership find the care of their elderly parents a more pressing issue than the care of young children.
- More elderly will continue to vote. Children as always will have to depend on others to represent them in the political sphere.

If we can leverage the resources, what will a system look like? How can the patches be put together to assure accessibility, affordability, quality and flexibility? It is not 1972 and it is unlikely that a single system can be superimposed. What role will the federal government take?

- Will in the year 2000, Iowa still limit eligibility for child care to families earning less than poverty level wages or Texas to those earning less than half the state's median income?
- Will Louisiana still not have licensing for child care?
- Will we be able to fill all the gaps in our system by the year 2000? Can we afford increased paternity leave, more infant, pre-school and school-age care?
- What role will the schools play in meeting child care needs? Will child care professionals and advocates and parents demand protection to ensure that child care that develops in the schools is sensitive to the needs of young children and their families? Will half day pre-school programs and kindergarten programs that end at 3 o'clock create an even younger group of latchkey children?
- If schools serve more four year olds, will Head Start begin to reach one and two year olds and play a stronger role in helping adolescent mothers? Will community based child care programs survive and flourish? How will family day care be affected?
- Will centers be able to leverage the resources to develop more infant care programs and will family day care providers receive support in caring for younger children?

- Will the federal government help to insure quality child care by providing financial incentives to states which meet model guidelines?
- Will training funds be available to help insure that child care is provided by skilled caregivers? What will CDA look like in the year 2000? Will the federal government continue to support the assessment and credentialing of child care workers or will CDA be phased out because the eliminations of federal support will increase the costs of credentialing beyond the reach of low salaried child care workers?
- Will increased child care in schools move child care salaries up or simply provide new job opportunities for teachers?
- Will the private sector be funding the bulk of Information and Referral programs? How will I&R be funded in areas with no employer interest?
- What will the role of the private sector be in the year 2000? Will they act as a lobbying force for increased public dollars in addition to putting in place more responsive family policies?

The questions are many and we have only touched upon a few. Many of the issues are difficult and will require complex negotiating and painful trade-offs. However, it is also a period of tremendous potential. A time for this country to dig in its heels and for the many desperate interests to join together and build the child care system that will insure a positive early education experience for all our children.

Section II:
Day Care Options

Introduction

Child care in America takes many forms. The child of a working parent may be cared for by someone employed to come to the parent's home each day. Or, the child may be taken to the home of a relative or friend during working hours. Another type of day care—family day care—generally refers to a setting in which an individual cares for several children in his/her home and charges a daily, weekly, or monthly rate. Restrictions may be placed on the ages of the children accepted and on the total number cared for at any one time. Most states require family day care homes to be registered or licensed, to uphold certain standards, and to be evaluated or inspected periodically.

Another option available to parents is the commercial day care center, where a relatively large number of children are grouped by age. Many such centers will not take children under the age of 18 months or 2 years. Some centers operate a kindergarten for 5 year olds and provide before- and after-school care for older children as well as transportation to and from the public schools in the area. Additional services that may be offered to parents, generally at additional cost, are dance and gymnastics lessons, computer instruction, field trips, and team sports.

The articles in this section address one or more of these options. The first, "Supporting Toddler Play," by Brenda Krause Eheart and Robin Lynn Leavitt, considers the day care needs of toddlers. It emphasizes that play should be the care around which a day care program for this age group is built. The authors offer guidelines for child care personnel as well as parents for providing a supportive environment that will facilitate play experiences and suggest ways to plan activities that enhance toddler play.

The next 2 articles in this section discuss the often overlooked problem of providing day care to school-age children, or after-school care. Marion R. McNairy, in "School-Age Child Care: Program and Policy Issues," gives some staggering figures on the number of "latchkey children" and the problems associated with unsupervised care of school-age youngsters. She describes the types of programs that could be offered as well as policy issues relating to facilities, administration, eligibility criteria, and licensing.

In "School-Age Child Care: In Support of Development and Learning," Peggy Lewis Nieting reiterates the need for care of this age group and discusses ways of meeting this need through various community organizations or through a link with the public schools. The major factor, however, is that the curriculum implemented be responsive to the developmental needs of older children.

Family day care, in which a limited number of children of any age group are cared for, usually in a private residential setting, is the topic of the next article. Diane Adams, in "Family Day Care Registration: Is It Deregulation or More Feasible State Public Policy?," looks at the complex, confusing, yet critical issue of licensing, registration, and/or certification of family day care homes. She offers some insight into the topic by defining the types of regulation in use and by discussing some of the problems with family day care. Her remarks are based on a comprehensive study, also by her, of regulation of family day care nationwide. The text of this study appears in Appendix A of this book.

Finally, how one group of parents set about fulfilling their day care needs is related in "Day Care and Community: The Necessary Partnership," by Aimee Nover and Ann Segal. The need for dependable and accessible day care prompted members of a Maryland community to work together to find a facility, locate funding, design a program, and select a professionally trained staff. The project, originally begun by parents, gradually evolved into one in which high school students, school personnel, and workers in the community began to invest their time and energies.

Supporting Toddler Play

Brenda Krause Eheart and Robin Lynn Leavitt

A re the staff in your program pressured to teach toddlers how to read or other similar but inappropriate skills? Have you been looking for some principles upon which to base your toddler curriculum? Staff and parents may want to share this brief discussion on the importance of play for toddlers.

* * *

Play is the central activity of childhood. For toddlers, play is the way they learn about themselves and their world. It is also the way they begin to master many fundamental physical, social, and intellectual skills and concepts. Trained staff in programs for young children recognize the importance of play in a young child's life, as did Hartley and Goldenson when they wrote that "play is not only the child's response to life; it is his life if he is to be a vital, growing, creative individual" (1963, p. 1).

Due to the extreme value of play for young children and rapidly growing numbers of toddlers in group programs, the role of the adult in facilitating quality play is increasingly important. Toddlers can experience high quality play if adults support the children's play, whether it is initiated by the children or planned by an adult.

Support play

The adult's primary responsibility in facilitating toddler play is to be a supportive participant. A supportive adult responds to a toddler's initiations in play by expanding the scope of the play while still allowing the toddler to take the lead. Adults tailor their behavior to the toddler's activity and respond thoughtfully and appropriately. In this way the adult helps the child move ahead in all areas of development. The following guidelines offer some suggestions for enhancing play in a supportive environment.

Guidelines for supporting play

1. Observe children's play. Through observation, adults assess children's development and learn about the uniqueness of each child. You may find that one child spends much time using table toys or that another changes areas rapidly. Keeping records of these behaviors can help you select activities and guide children's participation.

2. Take advantage of opportune moments for expanding children's play. You can help them elaborate on their play by suggesting new ideas or adding props to their play areas. Try to pick up on what a child says or does—ask open-ended questions, comment, or describe what the child is doing. For example, if two children initiate playing grocery store, an adult can offer props such as plastic fruit and vegetables or empty cereal boxes. Questions such as "Tom, I see that you are doing some shopping! What are you going to buy?" help children expand their dramatic play ideas on their own.

3. Encourage young children to explore and experiment with materials in their own ways with the least amount of direction. Once children are playing independently, avoid hovering or smothering them with attention. In the above example, the adult helped children set up the store and asked a question which related to their child-initiated play. Then she observed from a distance—they were barely aware of her presence!

4. Allow children to be as independent as they are able. You might be tempted to show a child which way a puzzle piece goes, but the value of a child's discovery is more important than a finished puzzle.

5. Avoid interrupting children's play unless absolutely necessary for a scheduled routine such as lunch or nap (in which case adequate warning should be given). Do not interrupt child-directed play for an adult-directed activity.

6. Let young children know you are interested in what they do by encouraging them to talk about their play. For younger toddlers with limited language, review their play aloud for them. They love to hear about themselves and your interest will thrill them! "Marcus is using the red marker. Look how he draws from one side of the paper across to the other. He makes fast lines! Now he's drawing slowly!"

7. Be available to children for assistance when needed. At least one adult in a team needs to maintain an awareness of the entire group, so children's needs can be met immediately.

8. Avoid needless conversation with other adults. Staff should be either involved with children during play or observing them.

Plan for play

In addition to following these guidelines, adults must plan to support children's play. First, staff should evaluate the physical environment. A good setting for toddlers is one that invites them to explore and manipulate materials on their own. Materials must be accessible to children, enabling them to pursue self-chosen activities. Play materials and their use by toddlers are periodically re-evaluated as the staff add to, rearrange, or change them.

Staff also plan for play by designing special experiences that toddlers cannot initiate on their own. These adult-initiated activities are based on the staff's daily observations of the children as well as on formal assessments. They also must meet the following criteria as outlined by Spodek (1977).

1. The activity *takes into account how toddlers come to know* or understand concepts and relationships. This allows children to learn through active experience and exploration. The staff ask themselves: Can children use more than one sense to examine materials? Can they manipulate them over time? Are they real and familiar?

2. The activity is *developmentally appropriate*, taking into account what toddlers know and can do while still exercising and challenging their emerging capabilities.

3. The experience is *worthwhile*. Children will use or gain skills that will transfer for later learning. The activity is not something simply to keep them busy or produce an end product.

Some examples of play activities appropriate for toddlers would be finger painting, dancing to records, playing lotto games, water play, and stringing large beads. These activities need close adult supervision for manageability and safety.

Staff can plan these activities in advance, except perhaps for the very experienced who have learned to initiate activities spontaneously, drawing from the wealth of ideas they have accumulated. At the Infant-Toddler Center (ITC) at the University of Illinois, the toddler staff meets weekly to discuss the experiences they would like to provide for the toddlers, based on their observations and assessments. A weekly plan summarizing these activities in one or two words is posted (see Table 1). These plans are kept on file, so staff can be sure they offer a variety of experiences.

Table 1. Weekly activity plan.

Day	Morning	Afternoon
Monday	finger painting	walk to flower garden
Tuesday	Playdoh lotto cards	easel painting
Wednesday	water play pegboards	dance with scarves to records
Thursday	wash vegetables for snack	string beads
Friday	musical instruments	paste tissue

Schedule for play

Despite all the convincing evidence we have that young children learn best through play, many adults equate planned activities with lessons. They set aside a separate part of the day for a learning period or lesson time. During this time, their planned activities are introduced. These activities are usually adult-directed. All of the children stop playing and participate. The activities are structured and formal with specific learning objectives in mind. They often require a completed product as evidence that the toddlers are learning. Unfortunately, the learning process becomes secondary to the end product.

While the *intent* of these lessons is to foster development,

the *method* is inappropriate for toddlers. When children are often asked to put away activities they are already engaged in, their self-chosen play becomes subordinate to adult-planned activities.

Introduce activities and materials enthusiastically.

Adult-imposed activities do not take into account how toddlers learn. Young children do not learn by quietly listening to adults, so what is taught is not likely to be internalized or remembered (Watrin and Furfey 1978). Toddlers' learning depends on the freedom to actively experience the environment.

In addition, adult-imposed activities can fail to account for individual differences in the capabilities and interests of the children. A group of children cannot be expected to learn the same thing, the same way, at the same time.

At the ITC, *child-directed play is the curriculum*, whether the play is initiated by a child or an adult. Consequently, the daily schedule does not include specific times for free play,

---

Guidelines for supporting toddler play

1. Observe children's play.
2. Take advantage of opportune moments for expanding children's play.
3. Encourage children to explore and experiment with materials in their own ways with the least amount of direction.
4. Allow children to be as independent as they are able.
5. Avoid interrupting children's play unless absolutely necessary for a scheduled routine such as lunch or nap (in which case adequate warning should be given).
6. Let children know you are interested in what they do by encouraging them to talk about their play.
7. Be available to children for assistance when needed.
8. Avoid needless conversation with other adults.

---

lessons, or teacher-planned activities. Instead, staff introduce most of their planned activities at opportune moments. For some activities, such as water play or Playdoh, materials are prepared early in the morning or during naptime. These activities are inviting play choices when the children arrive or awaken. An adult remains in the area to work with those children who choose to participate while other toddlers involve themselves in different play activities of their own choosing.

Some days the posted activities may not be introduced at all if adults follow the children's lead to determine when, what, and how to implement their planned activities. This example illustrates how an adult-initiated activity can be introduced.

The toddlers have been involved in the play of their choice since their arrival. Neil pushes a wheel toy, a few toddlers work puzzles in the manipulative area, Michael and Andy look at books by themselves, and two others help an adult fold the morning laundry. Amy quietly wanders about watching the others.

Gary aimlessly throws the farm animals he had been playing with across the room, and is redirected to the blocks by the adult. A few minutes later he pushes Amy. The floating staff member concludes that Gary might be bored, and that wandering Amy might be unable to make a play choice this morning. She invites both children to help her set up a crafts activity (the posted activity for the morning) in the art area. They help her put out paste and paper and sit at the table with her to make tissue collages.

Michael and Andy, finished with their books, notice Gary and Amy's involvement and join them. The other toddlers continue to play in their chosen areas. Later Gary leaves to play outside and Carin comes in to try the pasting.

No child's play was interrupted to make them participate in the pasting activity—children came to and left the activity as they wished. After introducing the activity, the adult's responsibility was to let the children direct the play and to support that play. There was no formal instruction. The paste and paper remained available for most of the morning, as some toddlers would come back a second time, until no more interest was shown. The adult then asked two children to help put the materials away and wash the table. They then helped her display the collages on the classroom walls.

Sometimes, if a toddler has not made a choice from the play activities available and resists adult suggestions, the adult can ask the toddler what she or he would like to do. Often this means being flexible enough to take out pegboards, lotto cards, or musical instruments although these activities were not originally planned. Being flexible encourages children's independence in making choices, gives them some control over their environment, and lets them know their choices are important. Also, children become more involved in play they have chosen themselves. The following guidelines will help staff implement their planned activities.

Guidelines for planned activities

1. Plan small group activities for no more than three or four toddlers at a time. When activities are more individualized, children spend very little time waiting. Interaction among children and adults is promoted in smaller group activities.

2. Allow children to do for themselves as much as possible, avoiding the temptation to make the activity easier for the adult by doing it for the children. When adults do almost all the cutting and pasting in crafts activities, for example, the value of the experience is lost for the children.

3. To prevent frustration and boredom, try not to expect too much or too little from the children. Toddlers can be messy, active, and protective of their toys and their space. At the same time, they can solve many of their own problems, are able to work on a project or activity of their own choosing for amazingly long periods, and can be responsible for returning materials to the proper place. Having appropriate developmental expectations regarding toddlers' behavior during planned activities is an extremely important quality for a good toddler staff member!

4. Allow children to make errors and trust that they can solve problems. Children learn from experimenting.

Thus, the process becomes more important than the solution or product. Be ready to help when needed, however, and encourage children to help each other. In addition, be flexible enough to incorporate children's playful, spontaneous ideas into any activity.

5. Plan for children to be actively involved in the activity. While toddlers may enjoy watching and listening to a limited extent, passive waiting is difficult for them. Be sure children are involved as much as they are able in all aspects of the activity, including preparation and cleanup.

6. Avoid dominating toddlers' play. Drilling, quizzing, telling children what to do, making too many suggestions, or criticizing makes children self-conscious and diminishes the value of play.

7. Introduce activities and materials enthusiastically. Prepare them so they are attractive and inviting to the children.

8. Avoid comparing one child's work to that of another. Comment, instead, on what they are doing. "I see you put your pegs all around the edges of the board." "You have covered your entire paper with purple paint!"

9. Be prepared to drop your plans, and instead, follow the children's lead, expanding on the play in which they are already involved.

Guidelines for planned activities

1. Plan small group activities for no more than three or four toddlers at a time.

2. Allow children to do for themselves as much as possible, avoiding the temptation to make the activity easier for the adult by doing it for the children.

3. To prevent frustration and boredom, try not to expect too much or too little from the children.

4. Allow children to make errors and trust that they can solve problems.

5. Plan for children to be actively involved in the activity.

6. Avoid dominating toddlers' play.

7. Introduce activities and materials enthusiastically.

8. Avoid comparing one child's work to that of another.

9. Be prepared to drop your plans and instead follow the children's lead, expanding on the play in which they are already involved.

Child-centered play

All of the guidelines presented here are based on the principle that the primary responsibility of adults, during both child- and adult-initiated play, is to allow the children to direct the play. Leading developmental specialists and theorists, including White, Brazelton, Piaget, and Erikson, suggest this approach to caregiving. Likewise, most professional texts in early childhood education suggest the importance of child-centered programs.

Play *is* the central activity of childhood.

Yet, perhaps in part because of the recent expansion of toddler group care and the criticism of education in general, we hear more and more about the lack of programs that are developmental and child-centered. For example, one mother wrote extensively about her difficulty in finding a child care center for her two-year-old which would "let children be kids" (Solovitch 1983). Documenting this trend has been the important and enlightening research of Suransky (1983). She is concerned that although childhood is a natural phase of life, we are eroding this life phase because of the social ideology of schooling which is embedded in many early childhood programs.

Why has this trend toward schooling and structure in toddler programs become so widespread? One reason is because growing numbers of parents want it. *Newsweek* (March 28, 1983) quoted one mother of a nine-week-old baby as saying, "There is so much pressure to get into college, you have to start them young and push them toward their goal." Early childhood program staff and directors can begin to reverse this trend if they recognize the extreme importance of play and provide parents with the evidence that documents it.

Play *is* the central activity of childhood. Once adults understand how toddlers play, plans can be made for both child- and adult-initiated play activities in a child-centered program. By following the guidelines presented here, adults will enter the toddler's world of play and develop quality programs and curricula that meet toddlers' developmental needs as they become creative, vital, happy individuals.

References

"Bringing Up Superbaby." *Newsweek* (March 28, 1983): 62–68.

Hartley, R. and Goldenson, R. *The Complete Book of Children's Play.* New York: Crowell, 1963.

Solovitch, S. "Why Won't Preschools Let Children Be Kids?" *The Washington Post* (May 1, 1983): B1–B2.

Spodek, B. "What Constitutes Worthwhile Experiences for Young Children?" In *Teaching Practices: Reexamining Assumptions,* ed. B. Spodek. Washington, D.C.: National Association for the Education of Young Children, 1977.

Suransky, V. *The Erosion of Childhood.* Chicago: University of Chicago Press, 1982.

Watrin, R. and Furfey, P. *Learning Activities for the Young Preschool Child.* New York: Van Nostrand Rheinhold, 1978.

School-Age Child Care:
Program and Policy Issues
by Marion R. McNairy

Child care for school-age children must grow to meet the increasing needs of families. McNairy talks about the interrelationships of program and policy issues connected with after-school care and the role of educators in partnerships with other concerned groups.

"2:30 p.m.—CALL PETER!" My child is coming home from school, and I am not there to greet him, to hear about his day, to supervise his snack, to make sure that he doesn't watch television all afternoon, to help him with homework and see that he gets outdoors for exercise. I am not at home because I am a working mother, and Peter is a *latchkey* child.

Our experience, Peter's and mine, is not a new phenomenon, nor is it unique. Historically, the need for child care for school-age children began in the late nineteenth and early twentieth centuries when patterns of child rearing changed as a result of the emergence and growth of industrialization and urbanization. After-school care developed as early as the mid-1890s. Later, the progressive education movement led to the establishment of summer *play schools* for low-income children. With the demand for a female work force during World War II the federal government subsidized care for school-age children, but government financial support, for the most part, declined after the war. The renewed interest in child-care services in the 1960s and 1970s provided only minimal advocacy for services for school-age children.[1]

Many contemporary parents have an urgent need for after-school care for their school-age children. Stroman and Duff, using the 1976 Census Bureau figures, indicate that nearly two million, or 13% of the children between the ages of 7 and 13 whose mothers work outside the home, cared for themselves.[2] Levine, et al., citing figures published in 1978 and 1980, reported that 25% of the children between the ages of 6 and 13 cared for themselves. They warned, however, that these figures were not an accurate assessment of current needs because the figures do not include a large population of five-year-olds who need after-kindergarten care.[3] They further noted that by 1990, 18 million children ages 6 through 13, and 1 1/2 million five-year-olds will need after-school care.

While the current and predicted needs seem staggering, the risks involved in leaving school-age children to care for themselves are frightening. Their feelings of loneliness, fearfulness, rejection, and alienation are accompanied by increased risks of accidents and sexual victimization, overexposure to television, exposure to drugs and alcohol, improper nutrition leading to obesity, peer pressure leading to vandalism and delinquency, and academic failure.[4] All this points to a need to examine issues in child-care services for school-age children so that educators can address policy and programming needs.

Program Issues

Program issues pertain to the on-site, direct delivery of services to children and include program goals for curriculum and staffing. Goals and services are generally based on whether the care is defined as *custodial* or *developmental*. Custodial care generally refers to minimal safety care for children, usually ignoring their social, emotional, and intellectual needs. Galinsky and Hooks warned that custodial programs could be used as repositories for children with attendant negative images of both the care and the children.[5] Hoffman, however, stressed the need for goals that focus on the developmental needs of school-age children. Such programs should provide children with the following opportunities:

- to gain self-respect,
- to mature to the child's own capacity,
- to be an integral part of the community,
- to make choices of friends and activities, and
- to have opportunities to pursue individual interests.[6]

The establishment of program goals leads to decisions about the curriculum of such programs. Some view after-school care as an opportunity to improve the academic achievement of school-age children. For example, the Children's Centers in California have been charged by state education personnel to participate in the development of a competency-based academic program, and Atlanta's Expanded Day programs for kindergarten children are used to reinforce concepts learned in kindergarten classrooms.[7] Others, however, feel that after-school care should not be an extension of the school day, but that there should be qualitative differences in the two programs. The local personnel of the California Children's Centers see academically oriented programs as being too restrictive, and the Brookline, Massachusetts Extended Day programs have defined curriculum as nonacademic activities such as arts and crafts, cooking, music, and athletics.[8]

A third approach to program curriculum is one in which academic skills are integrated with other activities. The curriculum in one New York City program, for example, includes experiential learning of skills, homework, sports, and ethnic activities.[9]

Issues surrounding goals and curriculum of after-school programs also lead to questions related to staffing, such as salary, roles, role ambiguity, and hiring practices. The major issue is that of criteria for staff selection. Two criteria predominate: 1) educational attainment accompanied by credentialing, and 2) experience in working with children.

The educational attainment criterion was described in both the California and Atlanta programs cited by Levine and in the New York City program cited by Galinsky and Hooks. In these three examples, teaching staff were divided into groups on the basis of educational attainment, with head teachers or teacher-administrators having the greatest amount of education. All three programs required a B.A. degree, but California programs require an additional fifth year of study in either early childhood education, elementary education, or multiple-subjects study. The Atlanta programs required staff to have had four years of teaching experience in addition to the degree. The second group of staff members in each of

Reprinted with permission from *Educational Horizons* 62 (2) (Winter 1984): 64–67.

> *"The use of public schools. . . . eliminates the need for after-school transportation; allows for the effective use of physical resources; and it encourages partnerships between community agencies and schools. . . . "*

these programs, noncredentialed personnel, were required to have extensive educational background in either child development or early childhood education.

The second criterion for selection of staff for after-school care focuses on experience and attitude as more important than educational attainment. The Brookline programs, for example, maintain that

a teaching degree is less important than experience working with children and a feeling by parents that they and their children would be comfortable with that person.[10]

This criterion would allow noncredentialed persons such as recreation workers to be an integral part of the staff.

If programs are geared toward academic achievement, staff selection would probably be based on educational achievement and proper credentials. If, on the other hand, developmental goals led to an enrichment curriculum, experience and attitude might be the more meaningful standard. Thus, the interrelationships between and among these issues must be considered in the delivery of after-school care.

Policy Issues—Facilities

In addition to program issues, a host of other issues exists that come under the heading of policy, issues that involve the administration of services and the types of facilities required to house the program.

Child-care facilities for school-age children can be defined as either in-home or center-based. In-home settings consist of either the child's own home, a family day-care home, or small group day-care homes. The advantages of in-home care, in addition to providing more flexible hours, are that children can remain in their own neighborhoods, attend local schools, utilize neighborhood resources, and function as if they were in their own homes. The disadvantages include potential inconsistency of caregivers, a general lack of recreational facilities for children, and minimal training and supervision of child-care workers as well as minimal pay and fringe benefits for them.

The four major subcategories of center-based care facilities are 1) nonprofit agency facilities serving youth, such as the YMCA, Boys' and Girls' Clubs, churches,

and park and recreation facilities, 2) day-care centers, 3) industrial facilities, and 4) public schools. The primary purpose of agencies serving youth is not to provide after-school care, although they are increasingly being used for that purpose. Such facilities do provide supervision of children in a safe environment; however, the use of several such facilities during a school week can lead to inconsistency of care. This fragmentation of care could lead to feelings of insecurity that could negatively affect a child's social and emotional development.

Day-care centers usually focus on child-care services for prekindergarten children, but they do serve some young school-age children. Levine, et al. noted that there are approximately 18,300 day-care centers in the U.S. serving 900 thousand children. Twenty-one percent of the total enrollment consists of five-year-olds, and 14% consists of children age six and over.[11] The advantages of day-care centers include licensed facilities (with a greater or lesser degree of regulation), opportunities for play with educational equipment, access to woodworking tools, opportunities to use recreational space and equipment, opportunities for peer interaction, and opportunities for supervised field trips.[12] Among the disadvantages are fewer opportunities for reflective thinking, for choice of friends, for creating one's own amusement, and for experiencing and learning from working in the house and sharing family life.

A third type of center-based facility is located at the parent's work site. Keyserling reported a program begun by the president of the Baltimore region of the Amalgamated Clothing Workers Union to provide child-care centers for workers.[13] Employers at five industrial locations endorsed the programs because they led to reduced employee turnover and absenteeism and to increased worker productivity. However, transportation of children to and from the work place is a major problem in providing after-school care and one reason why such services may not increase significantly in the near future.[14]

The fourth type of center-based care facility is located in public schools. The use of public schools solves several problems simultaneously. It eliminates the need for after-school transportation; it allows for the effective use of physical

resources; and it encourages partnerships between community agencies and schools for the development of new programs to meet children's needs.[15] On the other hand, some think that the joint use of school buildings could restrict child-care providers, that such use might lead to the implementation of academic programs only, that conflicts might arise between after-school care programs and school-related extracurricular programs, and that problems of responsibility for such necessities as janitorial services might occur.[16]

There are advantages and disadvantages to each type of facility. No single environment is right for every child. Diffendal summarized the need for multiple options by stating that

a school-age day-care program should be tailored to the specific needs of the population and community in which it will be located, making best use of resources to reduce costs.[17]

This statement, while summarizing the need for alternatives in types of facilities, also leads to the next policy issue, administration.

Policy Issues—Administration

Under the general heading of administration can be included the following topics: 1) operating agencies, 2) funding, 3) admission or eligibility criteria, 4) licensing, 5) parent involvement, and 6) scheduling.

During the debates on comprehensive child-care legislation during the 1970s, Albert Shanker, president of the American Federation of Teachers, proposed that the public schools assume prime sponsorship of child-care delivery systems in an effort to avoid duplication of services, conflicts of interest, and wastefulness.[18] In addition to providing a single delivery system, schools also had both space and personnel to provide needed services. Opposition to Shanker's position by the day-care community was based on fears that if the schools were to assume prime sponsorship, programming would be too academically oriented, personnel would lack appropriate training for total developmental needs of children, and parents would not be involved in decision-making processes. These differing points of view should not obscure the fact that there are other types of operating agencies

"With the reduction of federal monies to social service programs . . . sources of funds will be a major problem in the provision of after-school programs."

in addition to local school systems. These include city agencies for child development and family services, private nonprofit community day-care corporations, community centers, parent groups, and commercial agencies. The major issue concerning operating agencies, therefore, is whether there should be a single operating agency or multiple options for the delivery of school-age child-care services.

A second administrative issue is that of funding. A review of several sources reveals multiple sources of funding for child-care programs.[19] These sources include federal, state, and city funds, school district funds (including both inkind and direct cash contributions), parent fees (including cash payments on both a flat fee rate and on a sliding scale), and contributions by consortiums of industries. In most instances, the major source of funding has been federal grants, especially through Title XX funds. With the reduction of federal monies to social service programs in recent years, sources of funds will be a major problem in the provision of after-school programs.[20]

The issue of eligibility or admissions criteria is closely tied to funding, especially when federal money is involved. When programs are supported by Title XX funds, eligibility for admission to the programs is restricted to former, actual, or potential welfare recipients thus excluding families of other income levels from needed services.[21] The major issue in eligibility policies, therefore, is whether admission to after-school, child-care programs should be based on income alone or whether admission should be based on need.

A fourth policy issue is licensing, particularly licensing agencies. Day-care and educational programs require different licensing agencies with different criteria. Both Levine and Galinsky and Hooks cited instances where the same buildings met standards for licensing for educational programs but did not meet standards for licensing for day-care programs.[22] There is an obvious need to develop one set of licensing standards and designate a single regulating agency to apply them to a variety of after-school programs.

The last two policy issues are related to parent involvement in the operation of day-care services and scheduling. As stated earlier, a major fear about public schools assuming operation of child-care services was that parents would be ignored. The major issue in parent involvement seems to be one of control or the degree to which parents are involved in decisions about program, staff, and budget.

The final issue is that of scheduling of child-care services. When we first hear the term *after-school care,* we tend to think of the hours between the end of the school day and the return of parents to the home after work. However, when parents work, children are often left alone before school, during school holidays, and during extended school vacations. The issue, therefore, is whether child-care programs for school-age children are viewed as extended day programs or whether they are viewed more comprehensively.

Program and policy issues, although separated for purposes of discussion, are interrelated. Moreover, matters pertaining to policy can strongly affect program dimensions and vice versa. The many issues involved in child-care services for school-age children are indicative of the complexity of the issue. In addition, they point to ways in which educators can be directly or indirectly involved.

Implications for Educators

What is the role of educators in insuring that the needs of school-age children are met when the school door closes at the end of the day? All too often educators' only role is to provide direct services to children. If educators were placed in the broader context of social and political responsibility, they could be involved in the following ways. First, educators need to accept the idea that the need for child-care services for school-age children is a legitimate one, not likely to disappear. Second, educators need to acknowledge publicly that need through professional organizations and at local, state, and federal levels of government. Finally, educators can become advocates for the development and implementation of child-care

programs for school-age children in partnership with other concerned groups. Parents, religious organizations, schools, and other community agencies can work together toward reform that will lead to better conditions for school-age children. □

1. J. Levine, et al., "School-Age Child Care," in *Day Care: Scientific and Social Policy Issues,* ed. E. F. Zigler and E.W. Gordon (Boston: Auburn House, 1982): 457-475.

2. S. H. Stroman and R. E. Duff, "The Latchkey Child: Whose Responsibility?," *Childhood Education* 59 (1982): 76-79.

3. J. Levine, et al., "School-Age Child Care."

4. Ibid.; Stroman and Duff, "The Latchkey Child."

5. E. Galinsky and W. H. Hooks, *The New Extended Family: Day Care That Works* (Boston: Houghton Mifflin Co., 1977).

6. G. Hoffman, *School Age Child Care: A Primer for Building Comprehensive Child Care Services* (Washington, DC: Publication no. (SRS) 73-23006, 1972).

7. J. Levine, *Day Care and the Public Schools: Profiles of Five Communities* (Newton, MA: Education Development Center, Inc., 1978).

8. Ibid.

9. Galinsky and Hooks, *New Extended Family.*

10. Levine, *Day Care,* 58.

11. J. Levine, et al., "School-Age Child Care."

12. Hoffman, *School Age Child Care.*

13. M. D. Keyserling, "New Directions in Day Care Needs and Services," *Viewpoints in Teaching and Learning* 55 (1979): 66-74.

14. E. Diffendal, *Day Care for School-Age Children* (Washington, DC: Day Care and Child Development Council, 1974).

15. Levine, et al., "School-Age Child Care."

16. Diffendal, *Day Care for School-Age Children.*

17. Ibid., 25.

18. Levine, *Day Care.*

19. B. M. Caldwell, "Day Care and the Schools," *Theory into Practice* 20 (1981): 121-129; Diffendal, *Day Care for School-Age Children;* Levine, *Day Care;* M. Mayesky, "Extended Day Program in a Public Elementary School," *Children Today* 8 (1979): 6-9.

20. M. W. Edelman, "The 1982 Elections—Their Implications for Families and Children in 1983," *Young Children* 38 (1983): 3.

21. W. N. Grubb and M. Lazerson, "Child Care, Government Financing, and the Public Schools," *School Review* 86 (1977): 5-37.

22. Levine, et al., "School-Age Child Care; Galinsky and Hooks, *The New Extended Family.*

School-Age Child Care

In Support of Development and Learning

Peggy Lewis Nieting

A DEFINITION

SCHOOL-AGE CHILD CARE refers to programs that serve elementary school-age children (ages 6-12) before and after regular school hours and during the summer. These programs are primarily a service for (although not limited to) working parents who need an alternative to traditional home care for their children. Many parents' work schedules do not coincide with school hours. School-age child care programs support and supplement the family by providing care that promotes the child's physical, social, emotional and cognitive development through nurturing caregivers and a planned environment. All good programs share at least two features: they add to and strengthen the care and guidance provided by parents; they aim to provide experiences that encourage healthy growth of the child's body, intellect and personality (Cohen,. 1972).

Child care for school-age children may be seen in the light of broader societal objectives that include commitment to children's right to the kind of care essential for their best physical, social, emotional and cognitive development. To achieve this goal, it is important to promote community institutions that support family life and help children fulfill their potential (Cohen, 1972).

A NEED

In the United States, there are growing numbers of families in which either both parents work or the family is headed by a single working parent. A 1975 National Child Care Consumer Study reported that of 29 million children ages 6-14 in the continental United States, 18 million had mothers in the work force. Of this number, only 1.6 million were enrolled in before- and after-school child care programs (DHEW, 1976); less than 9 percent of U.S.

children ages 6-14 in need of adult supervision while their parents worked were enrolled in supervision programs. The majority of school-agers with working parents receive informal supervision from neighbors, participate independently in various community activity programs or remain totally unsupervised during after-school hours.

The reasons for this gap between need and availability of adequate care are many and varied. Federal efforts and funds for day care, as well as research, have focused on the preschool child (Diffendal, 1973). Programs for school-age children are limited, and when available are often undifferentiated from preschool programs with which they are linked. Economic factors play a large role. Parents with more than one child place priority on care for preschool children; older children are often considered capable of fending for themselves (Harris, 1977; Rodes, 1975).

However capable children are, preadolescents need much more than self-care and supervision. As Gardner expresses, "They need challenge, stimulation, resource material, ideas, people around them who know how to listen, and adults with whom to identify. They have talents and skills to develop, energy to put to use, and huge reservoirs of creativity which need tapping" (Boe, 1970). In short, children ages 6-12 have changing developmental needs. The kind of environment in which they live and learn will have an impact on their growth and development.

Finally, the elementary school-age child faces many potential social, emotional and health problems related to behavior and development: alcoholism, drug use, juvenile delinquency (average age of observable onset is 8), obesity, pregnancy, TV addiction (Bergstrom, 1977; Cohen, 1972). Many feel that increases in these problem areas may be attributed in part to lack of supervision. Child care supervision, peer and adult interaction, and activities that direct energies into positive channels could help the school-age child to avoid or effectively deal with these problems.

A LINKAGE

The Family

Two incomes have enabled a significantly large number of families, across all socio-economic levels, to maintain their standard of living. Mothers are both electing and being forced to seek employment outside the home. Although priorities have not necessarily changed, they are being more acceptably expressed in different ways. Some parents find that their children benefit greatly from the economic advantages, and increasingly the necessity, of additional employment. Others find they serve their children best when they are feeling peaceful within themselves. For many this involves employment outside the home and the belief that the quality of time spent with their children is more important for their children's development than the quantity.

With the increase in the number of single-parent families, many families must rely heavily on institutions outside the home for a variety of child care functions. For working parents, the schools represent not only educational care, but also child care during the parents' working hours. Too often, however, work schedules do not coincide with school schedules. School-age child care can provide care for these children before and after school, during school breaks and during the summer. By accommodating working parents' schedules and children's needs, child care programs supplement what a family can provide and thus preserve rather than destroy family life.

The School

Next to the family, the school is the central institution in children's lives through which they experience cognitive and affective learning. Child care can both supplement and complement the school's goals in education. While the school's major focus is on cognitive skills and related areas of developmental learning, child care can focus on social and emotional development, which affects formal learning.

While schools are available for only part of the day and year, child care can provide a quality environment during the remaining time. While schools provide mostly formal learning settings in which children are expected to conform to class needs, child care can offer more informal settings for affective and investigative learning geared to individual needs. Children are able to extend school learning in an atmosphere free of pressure to acquire specific skills on schedule. While school places more emphasis on skills than relationships, child care can place more emphasis on children's relationships with peers and adults. In all these areas, the child's education, in the broad sense of growth and development, supports and complements the school's goals.

Many people in both the public and non-public sectors of education advocate the linkage of school-age child care with elementary schools. Through sharing staff, facilities and children, they maintain, children, families, schools and communities all benefit.

Mary E. Mayesky (1980) reports that a child care program can have a positive impact on children's academic growth. The Phillips Extended Day Magnet, a school-age child care program in North Carolina, reported a statistically significant difference in reading and math performance at the end of a three-year period in children who attended the program, as compared with a comparable group of children who were not enrolled. She attributes this growth to the goals and design of the program—which included high-interest activity areas for cognitive, affective and psychomotor learning—and to qualified staff.

Mayesky concludes that the extended day program's non-threatening environment and the smaller adult-child ratio contributed to the children's achievement. Moreover, all activity centers included materials appropriate to the developmental levels of the multi-age groups, and concepts were expanded both vertically (in difficulty) and horizontally (for enrichment). While all school-age child care programs are not as structured in their "unstructure," quality programs contain many of this program's elements that contribute to academic growth in a supportive way.

Mildred Messinger (1980), a Berkeley, California, public school administrator, states that due to societal changes, "If your school doesn't have an after-school program, the likelihood that it will get one increases every day." She maintains that unused school facilities offer a solution to a growing need for after-school child care. Through facilitating school-based child care, she contends, an administrator creates good will for the school—particularly among working parents who are fast becoming a political force. It can soften the effects of declining enrollment and be a service to the community. Another benefit involves more comprehensive information about students through regular joint staff meetings and a shared set of student records. After-school child care, Messinger further claims, is a deterrent to vandalism. And, finally, children's learning is enhanced with on-site supervision, competent personnel, and a planned program of indoor and outdoor fun.

Jean Hawley (1980), Director of the Little School and School-Age Extended Day Program at Bryn Mawr School, Baltimore, Maryland, suggests that school-age child care programs are a logical extension of the goal of independent schools to provide a support structure for their constituent parents. Basic to a school-age child care program is the concept that children need a supportive environment in which to develop a sense of independence. The program offers free play, social interaction and directed group activity; the essential ingredient is the level of choice accorded to children within appropriate developmental levels.

Hawley states that the independent school community is challenged to support families in better and more realistic ways, to build a new constituency by extending programs. The question is not whether non-public schools should provide services to meet these needs, but when. "Independent schools are well advised to develop and provide programs before they find themselves playing catch-up to public facilities or reacting piecemeal to constituents' demands" (Hawley, 1980).

Indeed, school-age child care can be an effective link among child, family and school as it complements, supports and extends the school's educational purposes and supports the family in its education and nurturance of children. It can offer programs that encourage children to use their leisure time in a creative, self-fulfilling way. Moreover, learning situations are not confined to the classroom. Child care activities provide opportunities for creative play, which "is a developmental process during which children learn and grow through problem-solving. A series of successes in this kind of learning process brings with it increased confidence and self-esteem. These in turn strengthen emotional and intellectual readiness for further learning, informal or formal" (Eckstein, 1975).

The Community

School-age child care is not new. Recreation departments, libraries, museums, scouts, boys' and girls' clubs, 4-H, all have provided de facto child care after school, particularly for the older school-age child (Rubin, 1979). Although limited in service and scope for parents who need full child care services, these community programs play an important role in supplementing both family and school opportunities for children's healthy growth and development. School-age child care can supplement such programs by enabling children to use the opportunities for learning, friendship and fun which the community offers. Instead of stressing one building and one supervisor to "keep children out of trouble," child care can encourage independence appropriate to developmental levels by allowing children to make active and constructive use of the community in which they live (Boe, 1970; Cohen, 1972).

A RESPONSIVE CURRICULUM

The measure of a quality program is a flexible structure with appropriate activities that meet children's developmental needs. Throughout the program, there should be opportunities for healthy social, emotional, physical and cognitive growth. The program should promote a healthy self-image in children and allow them independence and self-direction appropriate to their level. A responsive curriculum is one of underlying structure: a relaxing yet stimulating environment should be available, in which children are free to make choices and to develop relationships with peers and adults. The quality of care will depend, of course, on how well the staff rises to the challenges and opportunities that arise daily.

Developmental Needs

According to Piaget (Mussen, 1979), the school-age child has entered into the concrete operational stage. Cognitive structures and the child's knowledge of the world are expanding. To develop these processes, the child needs activity and an environment upon which to act. This is also a stage of conscience and moral development in which moral realism yields gradually toward a consideration of others' needs. The child needs peer group interaction, with appropriate limits set by guiding adults who help model behavior. There are psychological problems specific to the middle childhood years. Erikson (Neugebauer, 1980) has described the school-age years as the period of industry vs. inferiority. During this period the child is attacking the tasks of acquiring a sense of industry, developing a sense of competence, fending off a sense of inferiority. The child needs opportunities to experience success, to experience a sense of industry, and to develop competence at both physical and intellectual levels. School-age children want and need to engage in real-life activities in a real world.

The Response

In considering the needs and problems of school-age children and the findings of several surveys of existing school-age programs, the following key characteristics of responsive school-age curricula have been identified (Neugebauer, 1980): providing opportunities for initiative; supporting children's sense of competence; supporting children's peer association; involving adults appropriately (as challenging role models actively involved in support and encouragement); complementing the schools; emphasizing recreational activities appropriately; involving children in the community.

A Model

Prescott and Millich (1974) did an extensive study of group child care for the school-age child and assessed what constitutes a quality program. They concluded that "Complex Activity Programs" best meet the developmental needs of school-age children:

This program provides non-nursery school activities which require initiative and encourage continuity. These activities are characterized by high adult involvement and know-how, good space and ample equipment and supplies. Work activities are also a part of these programs. The program, with the help of authoritative adult support, appears to develop a social system among children with responsibilities, obligations and a sense of belonging.

They found that the types of activities occurring most often in school-age programs (and the frequency observed) were:

Sports	18%	Construction	2%
Arts and Crafts	11	Reading	2
Games	10	Watching	2
Dramatic Play	9	Restriction	2
In Transition	8	Music/Dance	1
Exploring	7	Homework	1
Conversation	7	Eating	1
Doing Work	5	Listening	1
Horsing Around	4	Watching TV	1
Self Care	4	Other	3

Resources

Program and activity guides are helpful in any curriculum to focus thoughts and planning, spark ideas and point to other resources. In the field of school-age child care, until recently few such resources have been available. The following ones provide a wide range of helpful activity ideas and relative information:

Blau, Rosalie. *Activities for School-Age Child Care*. Washington, DC: National Association for the Education of Young Children, 1977.

Brown, Gayle. *Day Care for School-Agers, Parents, and Day Care Staff*. Austin: Texas State Department of Human Resources, 1977.

Scofield, Richard. *School-Age Notes*. Nashville, TN 37212: P.O. Box 120674.

CONCLUSION

School-age child care can support family, school and community by providing the services of a caring environment that fosters children's development and learning. Quality programs consider children's developmental and behavioral levels in planning appropriate activities which are both enjoyable and educational (in the broad sense of nurturing social, emotional, physical and cognitive growth). Unfortunately, many programs for school-age children are viewed by the staff as custodial—children are offered a "safe" holding place until parents arrive. Or school-age children are accepted into a primarily preschool child care or nursery center where activities are based on younger children's needs.

Those who work with school-age children in child care programs must be aware of children's developmental needs and the importance of the learning/nurturing environment. Such awareness is basic in planning appropriate and enjoyable programs. Quality developmental programs can become a reality for all children who require school-age child care. The need is great and the challenges many.

References

Bergstrom, Joan M., and Donna L. Dreher. *The Evaluation of Existing Federal Interagency Day Care Requirements: Day Care for the School-Age Child.* Washington, DC: DHEW, 1977.

Blau, Rosalie. *Activities for School-Age Child Care.* Washington, DC: National Association for the Education of Young Children, 1977.

Boe, Twyla. *Day Care for School-Age Children—A Linkage.* Denver, CO: Department of Social Services, 1970.

Brown, Gayle. *Day Care for School-Agers, Parents, and Day Care Staff.* Austin: Texas State Department of Human Resources, 1977.

Cohen, Donald J. *Day Care: Serving School-Age Children.* Child Development Series, No. 4. Washington, DC: HEW-OCD, 1972.

DHEW. *Statistical Highlights from the National Child Care Consumer Study.* Washington, DC: DHEW, 1976.

Diffendal, Elizabeth. *Day Care for School-Age Children. Final Report.* Washington, DC: UNCO, Inc., DHEW, 1973.

Eckstein, Esther. *Program Planning for 6-12-Year-Olds in Day Care Centers.* New York: Federation of Protestant Welfare Agencies, Inc., 1975.

Harris, Oliver C. "Day Care: Have We Forgotten the School-Age Child?" *Child Welfare* 58 (July 1977).

Hawley, Jean E. "Working Parents Face Schooling Decisions." *Independent School* (Dec. 1980).

Mayesky, Mary E. "Phillips Extended Day Magnet: A Successful Blend of Day Care and Academics." *Educational Horizons* 58 (Summer 1980).

Messinger, Mildred H. "Be a Hero: Provide Day Care." *The Executive Educator* (Mar. 1980).

Mussen, Paul. *Child Development and Personality.* New York: Harper and Row, 1979.

Neugebauer, Roger. *School Age Day Care: Developing a Responsive Curriculum.* Belmont, MA: Child Care Information Exchange, Jan. 1980.

Prescott, Elizabeth, and Cynthia Millich. *School's Out! Group Day Care for the School-Age Child.* Pasadena, CA: Pacific Oaks College, 1974.

Rodes, Thomas R., and John C. Moore. *National Child Care Consumer Study: 1975, Vol. 11. Current Patterns.* Washington, DC: UNCO Inc., OCD-DHEW, 1975.

Rubin, Victor, and Elliott Medrich. "Child Care, Recreation, and Fiscal Crisis." *Urban and Social Change Review* 12, 1 (1979).

Scofield, Richard. *School-Age Notes.* Nashville, TN 37212: P.O. Box 120674.

Family Day Care Registration: Is It Deregulation or More Feasible State Public Policy?*

by Diane Adams

Child care centers cannot accommodate the growing demand for child care, despite the rise in the number of centers from 18,300 full-day centers in 1976 (Coelen et al. 1978) to more than 50,000 full- and part-day centers in 1982 (Adams 1982). Family day care is therefore an important option for many families seeking child care. As early childhood educators we have a responsibility to keep informed about the rapidly changing family day care regulatory systems.

WHO USES FAMILY DAY CARE?

Families with infants and toddlers or school-age children, and families living in rural areas often select family day care, frequently because it is the only type of care available.

Child care centers are located primarily in urban areas, and even there the demand far exceeds the supply. Three million children under the age of three have employed mothers, yet there are only 122,000 licensed child care center spaces for very young children. While 14.5 million school age children have mothers who are employed, only 126,000 licensed spaces are available for these children (Children's Defense Fund 1982).

In addition to availability, cost and convenience factors are often cited by parents when they choose family day care.

HOW IS FAMILY DAY CARE REGULATED?

Unlike many group care centers, most family day care homes are not regulated by states, either because providers are not required to be licensed or they do not comply with the law. The definition of family day care varies widely, with minimum numbers of children cared for ranging from 1 to 6, and maximum numbers ranging from 4 to 15.

The type of regulation for family day care also varies. Licensing, certification, registration, and approval systems are common. It is little wonder that the public, policy makers, and providers themselves are confused! What is a *licensed home*? Is *registration* less regulation, or more? As states institute registration for family day care homes, will they undermine the more stringent center licensing system? The answers are not easy.

Regulatory terms often contradict common expectations. *Licensing* usually implies high quality to the public. For example, a licensed physician must have long years of training and pass a state examination. In child care, however, a license is simply a *permission to operate* after basic minimum legal requirements are met. In general, the group care or family day care facility is licensed rather than an individual. Family day care providers are usually licensed for their residence. If the provider moves, most states require a new license. Thirty states now license family day care homes (Adams 1982).

Registration is a more recent regulatory concept (Class 1980; Morgan 1982). Some common elements in registration include listing names with a central agency, provision of parent/consumer information, and spot-check monitoring for compliance with standards. In the 15 states that use registration, there are widely discrepant registration procedures.

● In Nebraska, a family day care license is required for anyone caring for children from more than

---

*Note: The text of *National Survey of Family Day Care Regulations: Summary of Findings,* from which some information reported in this article is taken, is reprinted in Appendix A of this book.

Reprinted by permission from *Young Children* Vol. 39, No. 4 (May 1984): pp. 74–78. ©1984 by the National Association for the Education of Young Children, 1834 Connecticut Ave., N.W., Washington, DC 20009.

one family. The licensing law is known as registration and there are standards for compliance.

- In North Carolina, providers caring for children from two or more families must register with the state, but there are no standards. Homes caring for children whose care is subsidized must meet certification requirements.
- In Texas, providers caring for from one to six children must register. Standards are available in English and Spanish.
- In Oregon, registration is voluntary for providers caring for fewer than five full-time children (Adams 1982).

In some states, registration is *more* regulation because formerly unregulated providers now must register. In others, licensing has been converted into registration, with little change in preinspection visits, fire safety requirements, and state monitoring. Information from pilot registration projects in states such as Texas, California, Michigan, Ohio, and Wisconsin may not be comparable due to the differences in the registration system.

Certification is the fiscal monitoring required by a funding source. States are required to use *certified* care when they purchase child care for low-income families through the Social Services Block Grant. States base certification on their state licensing or registration standard, or some other standard, because there are no federal standards. Five states regulate only those homes certified for subsidized care.

Why some homes are not regulated

Exemptions from licensing/registration rules account for some unregulated homes. Many state regulations apply only when a minimum number of children are cared for (see Table 1), so homes caring for fewer than this minimum number of children need not comply. Exemptions for the provider's own children and relatives' children are common.

Ignorance of state laws also contributes to a relative lack of regulated homes. Few states widely publicize their child care rules. In most states, child care licensing/registration is administered in departments of public welfare—an unfamiliar agency to many parents and providers.

Fear or defiance of the law are major reasons for noncompliance. Some providers may fear the possible intrusion of licensing or sanitation inspectors, some are reluctant to report child care income, and others genuinely believe that child care laws don't apply to their homes. Stringent licensing systems help reinforce these attitudes.

The rising sense of professionalism among family day care providers, encouragement from early childhood professionals, and consumer awareness

have led to regulation of about one-half of the family day care homes in some communities. However, although regulated family day care homes are more accessible to parents, there are fewer than 150,000 licensed or registered homes (and an unknown number of certified homes) in the United States (Adams 1982).

Table 1. Summary of number of children enrolled when family day care requirements must be met based on type of regulation (Adams 1982).

Number of states by type of system

Minimum number of children	Licensing	Registration	License & Register	No* system
1 or more	16	9	2	5
2, 3, or 4	9	3	1	-
5 or 6	5	-	-	-
Total	30	12	3	5

*Except subsidized care.

Changes in state and local systems

Controversy, heated debates, threats to remove licensure altogether, and misunderstanding surround state family day care regulation changes. New Jersey, a state that only regulates homes in which child care is purchased, has had several bills introduced to regulate all homes caring for fewer than six children. In Iowa, a number of attempts have been made to make the current registration system mandatory. Rhode Island has drafted registration guidelines, while in Ohio registration legislation has failed at least twice and Idaho is attempting to make voluntary licensing for homes mandatory.

California's proposed licensing cuts were reinstated only with the concerted efforts of advocates, parents, and providers, but a hiring freeze may hamper the efforts of licensing workers to carry out their responsibilities.

Texas recently reduced its list of registered providers from 18,000 to 10,000 when it verified active registered homes.

How does this dizzying array of requirements affect the quality of care for children?

DOES REGISTRATION WORK?

Unfortunately, most states do not use clearcut policy goals as a basis for instituting licensing or registration systems, so neither licensing nor registration has been perfected. The success of a registration system depends upon informed parents. Yet in many states using registration, copies of the standards are difficult to obtain or are in short supply. Many parents are confused about exactly what type of family day care is supposed to be regulated. In some communities, the Child Care Food Program is a prime impetus for following regulations, while in others, providers consider that program to require too much paperwork, and fail to have their family day care homes regulated.

When good forms of registration do occur, they can lead to further improvements in our child care service system. Any regulation that screens providers and requires even minimum health and safety standards serves as some form of protection for children and may increase professionalism. The increased visibility improves parental access and helps improve the whole child care delivery system. Regulated providers usually have greater access to information and referral services, food and nutrition information, and perhaps training. However, an invisible registration system cannot be effective, and states must make continuing efforts to inform consumers about child care regulations.

Deregulation has been an issue in many states, but there is no evidence that children need less protection now than in the past. There are more cases of child abuse and neglect. Parents are turning to regulatory agencies with complaints and concerns. As more new centers and homes emerge to meet the growing demand for child care, effective regulation remains a critical form of consumer protection.

What type of regulation will protect the most children and enable the most family day care providers to legally carry on their work? Will strict licensing rules with many exemptions accomplish any more than a simplified licensing system (registration) which has standards that are widely known about by parents? What is a feasible state child care regulatory policy? The goal of each state—in the absence of federal standards—should be to *improve* licensing, not simply deregulate child care.

REFERENCES

Adams, D. *National Survey of Family Day Care Regulations, Statistical Summary.* 1982. (ERIC Document Reproduction Service 220 207)

Children's Defense Fund. *America's Children and Their Families: Key Facts.* Washington, D.C.: Children's Defense Fund, 1982.

Class, N. "Some Reflections on the Development of Child Day Care Facility Licensing." In *Advances in Early Education and Day Care,* ed. S. Kilmer. Greenwich, Conn.: JAI Press, 1980.

Coelen, C.; Glantz, F.; and Calore, D. *Day Care Centers in the U.S.: A National Profile 1976–77.* Vol. III. In *Final Report of the National Day Care Study.* Cambridge, Mass.: Abt Associates, 1978.

Morgan, G. "Regulating Early Childhood Programs in the Eighties." In *Handbook of Research in Early Childhood Education,* ed. B. Spodek. New York: The Free Press, 1982.

DAY CARE AND COMMUNITY:
The Necessary Partnership

by Aimee Nover and Ann Segal

The Clara Barton Center for Children in Cabin John, Maryland was established to meet the expressed needs of the community for flexible, developmental day care. It has, from its inception, mobilized and utilized the resources of the family, the neighborhood, the community at large and the county (including both the public school system and the county government). Such aspects of the center's operation as funding, policy making and philosophical orientation are all a direct result of community influence and direction.

Responding to A Community Need

Cabin John and Bannockburn are older, "close in" neighboring communities in Montgomery County, Maryland, a suburban area bordering Washington, D.C. As parents of young children, and professional educators, we were aware of the lack of alternatives to existing child care programs in that area: nursery schools which operated five mornings a week, family day care or private babysitting arrangements. We undertook an informal survey of parents of preschoolers in the neighborhoods and found a high demand for flexible (full- and/or part-time) child care in a stimulating, nurturing (as opposed to custodial) environment which would be financially accessible to residents of both Cabin John and adjacent neighborhoods.

Involving Residents

Members of an *ad hoc* board of directors, drawn from interested community leaders, representatives of community organizations and parents, provided specialized knowledge and expertise to help us formulate plans. A lawyer volunteered his services to establish the center as a non-profit organization, draw-up bylaws and articles of incorporation, advise us on such matters as tax status, zoning and liability, and to generally function as legal counsel. Two community residents familiar with federal regulations informed us about day care staffing, policies and programs and helped us contact supportive organizations and advisory groups.

A child psychiatrist and a psychiatric social worker with training in child development and experience with day care programs helped us set policy and program goals which were both realistic and sensitive to the emotional, social and psychological needs of young children. A

pediatrician helped us formulate measures to ensure the health and safety of children in the program (and later served as the center's pediatrician). The president of the local elementary school PTA offered her perspective and an engineer helped us plan for the acquisition and renovation of physical equipment.

Finding A Facility

A day care facility must meet both the requirements of the program and the stringent state and county licensing standards in terms of number of square feet per child, number of accessible exits, location of rooms, adequacy of toilet facilities, etc. Consideration of facilities commonly used for day care—rooms in an office building or church, a converted home or store—did not yield any feasible possibilities in our area of the county.

Our search, however, coincided with the imminent closing, due to declining enrollment, of the Clara Barton Elementary School. The space available in the former kindergarten and primary wing of the school meshed with our requirements: bright, spacious ground-floor classrooms, each with one door leading directly to the outside and a second door opening onto a central hallway; ample, low shelving, a small-scale drinking fountain and a sink in each room; and a children's bathroom. The school, in a lovely wooded setting, also had a playground with both grassy and black top areas. Only minimal adjustment was needed to make the space suitable.

The location was also ideal. The elementary school which would be absorbing the Cabin John children was located in Bannockburn, and closing of the Clara Barton school would deprive Cabin John residents of a neighborhood school. Housing the center in Cabin John afforded an excellent opportunity to bring together children and families from both communities. The Cabin John community was supportive, for residents wanted to ensure that their building would be used to benefit the community.

Our major task was to obtain school board approval to use the space in Clara Barton for a day care center. We submitted a formal proposal requesting the use of three classrooms and the outdoor playground.

Although there were a few preschool programs in functioning elementary school classrooms, there was no precedent for housing a day care facility in a

closed school. Since declining enrollments were projected for many close-in Montgomery County schools, with the possibility that many schools might be closing in the future, the Clara Barton decision would have far-reaching implications.

While awaiting action by the school board, we solicited and received support in the form of letters and phone calls to school officials and board members from citizen groups and scores of individuals. We believe this support was a major factor in encouraging a positive decision on our behalf.

In June 1975, 15 months after the conception of our original plans for a neighborhood day care center, we were granted permission to use the space requested. (Subsequently, we were also allotted a fourth classroom and small office.) Initially no rent was charged (later we paid a minimal fee between 5:00 and 6:00 p.m. when the building was not normally heated) and, in this manner, our program was subsidized. We remained, however, a private, independent agency—and the school board's ruling set a precedent for a number of independent centers that are now operating either in closed elementary schools or in empty classrooms of functioning schools.

Preparing the Center

So many months were spent on theoretical planning that we were anxious to begin preparing our space for the children. The first task was to furnish and equip one classroom on a limited budget. Community residents made this possible by donating equipment, toys, books and furniture—and many services. One neighbor offered to do accounting and bookkeeping and two women, experienced nursery school teachers, volunteered to work in the classroom once a week to free teachers for staff meetings. In-service workshops in art, music and dance were offered by neighborhood professionals.

Obtaining Financial Support

Since the center is committed to serving children regardless of ability to pay—about one-quarter of our families receive some form of subsidy—additional funds were needed to supplement tuition payments. The center was not eligible for Title XX funding because we did not plan to provide a hot lunch. (The center does not have kitchen facilities and, rather than voting to have catered lunches, the board chose to ask children to bring lunch from home, with the center providing milk and snacks.)

A square dance and auction, now annual events, raised $1,200 and this sum, together with a $1,000 interest-free loan, provided our seed money. Local banks, businesses and merchants contributed cash and/or goods and services for the auction. In addition, individual donations specifically designated for the scholarship fund were received. As a result of such community participation, the center has never had to refuse an eligible child because of inability to pay and a broad socioeconomic and cultural mixture of children has been maintained.

While this initial money enabled us to begin operation, we realized that projected costs would substantially exceed this sum. The ongoing expenses of salary, supplies, food, equipment, insurance, repairs and subsidizing scholarships would totally exhaust our regular income. We needed capital for equipping the other classrooms, for playground equipment and a fence, for repairs and for purchasing a minibus to provide transportation, an essential need of many families.

A community resident suggested that the center investigate the possibility of obtaining a Community Development Block Grant from the Department of Housing and Urban Development (HUD), even though HUD was not known as a source for day care funding. Block Grant funds are provided by HUD to local governments for physical improvement of low- to moderate-income areas. Such grants had been awarded to Montgomery County for road and sewer construction, urban renewal and transportation services. The request for funds for physical equipment for a day care center, however, was unprecedented and we needed to demonstrate that the center was eligible as an essential community development activity.

Community residents who had had experience in writing grant proposals assisted one of the directors in preparing the center's proposal. The amount of $23,000 was requested to purchase equipment and a minibus and to pay a partial year's salary for a driver-recruiter for the center.

The proposal was submitted, together with more than 50 letters of support from all area citizen associations and many individuals. In addition, all of the elected officials whom we approached—county, state and national—wrote to the county government to indicate their support. When the proposal was presented at the Montgomery County Council hearing, 30 area residents—the majority of those present—appeared on our behalf. Testimony was presented by the heads of two neighborhood citizen's organizations, two center parents and the president of our Board of Directors. Community members contacted almost all of the 32 members of the county-wide Citizen's Advisory Panel to personally request approval of the proposal. Community efforts were constant throughout the entire process, which took nine months from the initial application to receipt of the first funds.

The grant of $20,000 was used to purchase a minibus and indoor equipment. Funds were also used to enhance the playground and provide an enriched outdoor environment not only for the center but for all of the neighborhood children. As a consequence of the grant, funds no longer need to be deflected for equipment and fund-raising efforts can now be directed toward supplementing tuition.

The Day Care Program

The Clara Barton Center for Children—a non-profit, non-sectarian facility—opened in December 1975. Three classrooms serving a maximum of 47 children at one time are now is use, together with a common room for group activities.

The program, planned and carried out by a professional staff trained in early child development, is designed so that the developmental needs of individual children as well as the group may be met. The specific goals set for each child include the following: to acquire a sense of identity and feeling of self-worth; to develop self-control, new skills and an increasing sense of independence; to function successfully as a group member; and to develop a sense of responsibility for himself and for others.

Each room contains a defined area for dramatic play, block building, arts and crafts, water play, table games, a cozy area and private nooks. The daily program involves music, storytelling, outdoor play and work with a wide variety of materials and objects to promote cognitive development. Self-initiative, independence and problem solving are encouraged as the child works within this setting at his or her own pace.

Staff-child ratio varies from 1:4 to 1:7 according to the children's age level and the time of day. Developmental level as well as chronological age is taken into account in each child's placement. A special effort is made so that siblings can interact, even if they are not in the same class, and there are opportunities for children to visit other rooms so they may benefit from mixed aged grouping.

Family Involvement

Our approach is to deal with the child not in isolation but as a member of the family unit. From the time the child is introduced to the center, parents and center staff work cooperatively.

Parents of children who are being considered for admission are required to tour the center and observe the classrooms. They meet with one of the directors to discuss their particular needs and to determine whether our program can successfully serve their child. After a child is accepted the teacher makes a home visit. We consider this visit (which is not an interview but rather a means of introducing the child to the teacher) imperative for a healthy transition between home and center, even if the child has had previous school experience. Thus, the teacher is already acquainted with a child before he or she enters the center, and the child knows something about the center's routine and can anticipate certain activities. No demands are placed on the child during the home visit; if he or she is reticent the teacher chats with the parent.

Parents or someone to whom the child is close (a grandparent or other relative, a family friend or a housekeeper) are required to remain with the child the first two days (which are always short days) and to maintain a flexible schedule for the ensuing week so that they can be supportive and available to the child at the center, if necessary. During this transition time, teachers talk with parents daily about their child's adjustment.

Parents, even those on rigid work schedules, have been very cooperative, either coming themselves or sending a surrogate, when they are made aware of our belief that this procedure will help to foster a positive separation experience. Additional preparation consists of obtaining the child's physical and developmental history and other pertinent data. This careful intake procedure has proved worthwhile in building mutual trust, cooperation and open communication between families and the center.

Parents As Policy Makers

The *ad hoc* board decided that parents should not only influence policy but that they should, in fact, have more authority than any other single group. Thus, eight out of 15 board members are parents. This representation ensures that parents' values will be uppermost in the minds of those who are directly responsible for the care of their children. The staff is ultimately accountable to the Board of Directors.

Parents and other family members are encouraged to participate in center activities. They can provide service to the center (often to help defray tuition cost) in a variety of ways—building and maintaining equipment, performing secretarial tasks, supplying special resources and acting as drivers or shoppers. Parents are also welcome in the classroom whenever their schedules permit to share special skills, assist the teachers or simply to visit and observe.

Parent-teacher conferences are scheduled regularly throughout the year, and conferences are also held at the request of a staff member or parent. Daily communication, however brief (exchanging information when a child is dropped off or picked up, for example), is encouraged.

The center maintains a library of books on child development and parenting for loan to parents. Parents are also welcome to attend our in-service workshops, conducted by specialists in such areas as gymnastics, music, first-aid, and the emotional development of young children. Health and mental health consultants are available to staff members and parents, and referrals to outside specialists and agencies are made when necessary.

This year, in response to parents' requests, special meetings around topics in which parents expressed particular interest are being held. The first, conducted by a child psychologist, a teacher and a pediatrician, focused on limit setting and discipline. Other sessions will be devoted to discussion of coping with common fears of childhood and aggressive behavior in young children.

Working with Community Agencies

We learned of a training program for day care teachers sponsored jointly by the Montgomery County Health Department (which licenses day care centers) and Antioch College and offered the use of the center as an observation site. Twice a week students observe the center's activities and teachers and then discuss their observations in class.

As an unanticipated benefit, students in the course devoted two Saturdays assisting our staff in making physical improvements to the center. One workshop dealt with ways to improve the physical layout of a classroom; the second focused on ways to enhance the playground by installing inexpensive equipment made from recycled materials.

The center currently employs as assistant teachers three women who have completed the day care teachers' course.

Other Support

After noticing a number of playground structures in the area built from recycled telephone poles, we called the Chesapeake and Potomac Telephone Company to find out how to obtain poles for our use. The company's community relations department arranged to have the poles delivered to us—and then agreed to construct a fort, free of charge, from the staff members' design.

Relationship with County Schools

We have maintained and expanded our relationship with the Montgomery County Public Schools. In response to parents' needs for after-school care, children are now bussed to the center from neighborhood kindergartens. Center staff members have developed a close relationship with the kindergarten teachers and, with explicit parental consent, share concerns and exchange information about the children with them. Through this interchange, each program works to enhance the other.

The center staff can also help to identify potential developmental problems of pre-kindergarteners and recommend specific evaluation and/or treatment procedures.

Students from county high schools have also become involved in the center program. A former member of our board, who is an engineer, told us of the Construction Trades Program, a part of the school's Industrial Arts division, in which high school students taking woodworking and masonry classes are as-

signed to work projects commissioned by community groups. Through this program students constructed needed equipment—toy stoves, refrigerators, sinks, hollow wooden blocks, storage cubbies—designed by staff members. There was no labor charge to the center, which purchased the materials, and the high school students participated in a practical learning experience.

The culmination of this joint project was the construction of a massive outdoor climber with slide and multi-level platforms. When the high school students came to install the climber they were greeted by an enthusiastic group of preschoolers who, after watching the building process with fascination, hosted a party for the students and served cookies and brownies which they had baked.

Another dimension of teenagers' involvement with children at the center is our practice of employing, as part of their high school work-study program, students who have completed the Parent-Child training course, which includes an internship in the high school laboratory nursery school. The center provides employment and training under master teachers; the students contribute their special skills and youthful enthusiasm. This job opportunity offers students a chance to apply the principles learned in their courses to the pragmatic tasks of child care, and it contributes as well to their training as prospective parents.

Conclusion

We believe that child care is a social responsibility: families need assistance and support in childrearing, and communities need to feel responsible for the care of the young. Thus, to truly fulfill its function a day care center should operate as an agent of the family and as an integral part of the community. This is possible only when the family and community work cooperatively with the center in a partnership in which responsibility, commitment and investment are shared by all participants. ∎

Section III:
Employer-Sponsored Day Care

Introduction

Employer-sponsored day care is becoming increasingly more popular. It is certainly an attractive option for parents for several reasons: It usually eliminates an intermediate and often out-of-the-way stop on the way to work; perhaps even more important from the parent's perspective, it keeps the children physically near during the working day. Of course, there are employer benefits as well. Ranking high among them are reduced absenteeism among employees as a result of the elimination of problems related to finding and keeping adequate child care. In addition, the knowledge that one's offspring are close at hand in case of illness or emergency makes it easier for the working parent to devote more of his/her energies to the job.

The articles within this section discuss the advantages and disadvantages of employer-sponsored day care and describe actual programs that have been sponsored at or near the job site by the employing agency. The first article, "Schools in the Workplace" by Judith P. LaVorgna, reviews the forces that have prompted this movement nationwide and describes some of the forms that preschool care in the workplace is taking. The author also takes a look at the long-range effects of employer-sponsored day care on the day care field in general.

Marce Verzaro-O'Brien, Denise LeBlanc, and Charles Hennon offer another perspective on the topic in their article, "Industry-Related Day Care: Trends and Options." Their discussion of the role of labor and business in the sponsorship of group day care draws from information gained from surveys of industries that now have or at one time provided day care services. The last part of the article focuses on the idea of early childhood educators serving in the role of resource person for businesses contemplating child care program sponsorship.

In "Employer-Sponsored Child Care on the Rise," Rick Graser explains the types of family-oriented benefits that can and are being provided by many companies. The efforts of the Appalachian Regional Commission (ARC) toward promoting employer-sponsored child care are detailed, along with the particulars of 5 grants awarded to encourage the establishment of child care services in Appalachia.

"Peace of mind" and "convenience" are 2 terms used to describe the feelings of employees talking about a day care center in the hospital in which they work. Carolyn Reece, in "Bringing Children To Work: A Hospital Day Care Center," discusses the many positive effects of having employees' children in an on-site day care program. The reasons behind the development of the program as well as some of the steps toward making it a reality are shared.

The final article in this section, "Child Care At Conferences: A Family Approach," reflects a seldom addressed need of some working parents. The author, Julie Carvalho, relates the experiences of one organization in providing day care services at a national training conference in order to attract participants who are not "childfree." Various aspects of providing this type of service are discussed under the headings of cost, location, insurance, and safety and health. Suggestions are given regarding other concerns such as staffing, activities and ways to involve parents.

Schools in the Workplace

by Judith P. LaVorgna

U.S. businesses and industries are beginning to offer child care as an employee benefit. Ms. LaVorgna examines the causes of this development and discusses what it means for other kinds of preschool education.

Behind the hospital, next door to the computer factory, inside a downtown office building, and on the second floor of an urban parking garage, U.S. children are going to preschool. School bells can be heard today in banks, warehouses, union offices, and retail stores. From ages six weeks to 5 years, U.S. children are going to preschool — at work.

Child-care centers in the workplace are springing up across the nation. In fact, this development has occurred so quickly that no comprehensive list of existing facilities is available.[1] But there are now 6.8 million children under the age of 6 who have working mothers, and these youngsters are vying for slightly more than one million spaces that are currently available in licensed child-care facilities.[2] As more women seek the satisfactions afforded by careers, as economic conditions make the two-paycheck family the norm, and as the number of single-parent families grows, the need for child-care facilities will be even greater. Therefore, industries and other institutions have begun to offer child care as an employee benefit.

Of 41 hospitals in southern Florida, for example, 15 either have or are now planning child-care facilities or other kinds of child-care options for employees.[3] Nor is Florida unusual in this respect. St. Francis Hospital in Hartford, Connecticut, and Memorial Medical Center in Long Beach, California, are representative of the other hospitals from coast to coast that have developed and implemented child-care facilities for employees' children. The allied health professions, with their critical need for personnel with special skills and training, are probably establishing a precedent that other employers will soon follow.

Throughout the U.S., a wide variety of workplaces already offer child-care facilities. These businesses and industries include many household names. Stride-Rite, Connecticut General Life Insurance, Intermedics, the Amalgamated Garment Workers Union, Welch Foods, Whirlpool, Texas Instruments, Playboy Resorts, and the Emperor Clock Company are but a few of the firms that now provide this new kind of employee benefit.

The reasons that cause corporations — both public and private — to become involved in child care are as many and as varied as the programs themselves. Local competition for a limited labor force and union demands are two contributing factors. For other institutions, such as the Mount Sinai Medical Center of Greater Miami, a child-care center serves not only to recruit but also to retain skilled employees. The center functions in this case as a family support system; the presence of children, in turn, humanizes the sponsoring workplace.[4]

In other instances, on-site or contracted child-care centers or child-care voucher systems allow employers to arrange around-the-clock work schedules for personnel with special skills. Work and child care are no longer mutually exclusive domains, as the workplace begins to take human needs into account. For still other industries, provision of child care is an attempt to enhance employees' productivity by reducing absenteeism and tardiness and by increasing morale and on-the-job performance.[5] It is too early to tell if some combination of these factors is causing companies to offer child care — or if the voices of economically beleaguered families are finally being heard.

One other factor also seems to be playing a vital role in the establishment of child-care facilities: money. Costs vary with location, educational programming, and staffing patterns. However, depending on the individual corporate structure, some of the expenses incurred in developing such a facility will — and do — become business-related tax deductions. Deficits from initial start-up costs (including construction, furnishings, and equipment) can be deducted in a variety of ways.[6]

At the same time, parent employees, who generally pay a share of child-care costs (often through payroll deductions), are able to recapture a portion of these moderate fees through annual income tax deductions for child care.[7] Although many employees may not realize this, most employers who provide child care

also subsidize the costs to some degree. The major financial burden remains with the employer, and most are apparently willing to pay the price.

A particular business or industry may choose to renovate existing space, construct its own free-standing facility near the workplace, construct a building with philanthropic funds, develop a voucher (or purchase-of-service) agreement with local child-care centers, or contract with one of the growing number of providers (such as Kinder-Care or Gerber) that build and manage such facilities. But the fact remains that these corporate options for the first time place children at or near the bottom line of corporate budgeting.

Industrial child care in the U.S. had a somewhat unsavory beginning. In 1910 child-care centers in factories apparently exposed employees' children to the same unsanitary and unhealthy conditions that their elders faced. The 1940s brought the Lanham Act, which funded community child-care programs for the children of Rosie the Riveter. Great Society funding brought Head Start in the Sixties. From these antecedents came today's employer-sponsored child-care movement. Given current economic conditions in the U.S. and the constantly increasing numbers of women entering the labor market, the 1980s should see even more corporate involvement in providing child care for the some 10 million preschoolers who will need such care at some point during the next eight years.[8] In fact, when Wheelock College and the Boston University School of Management co-hosted a conference on "New Management Initiatives for Working Parents" in 1980, some 33,000 invitations were mailed to U.S. corporations.[9]

A new and large-scale school system is unfolding before our very eyes. This school system is currently fragmented in terms of location and lacks a systematic communication system. With the establishment of a professional organization or agency to oversee it, however, this system could eventually provide most of the prekindergarten educational services in the U.S. If certain criteria are met, this new school system in the workplace, geared to providing care and education for infants, toddlers, and nursery schoolers, may even come to challenge the public school in the quality, nature, and delivery of services.

Among these criteria are the maintenance of a corporate conscience in dealing with employees and their young children. Industries must also extend to these preschool programs the positive benefits of quality and product control, performance-based staff and student evaluations, and management by measurable objectives. Young children must be allowed to grow and learn in carefully prepared environments staffed by highly qualified personnel. The adult/child ratios must be appropriate. The diagnostic procedures of early childhood education must be incorporated into these programs, along with remediation for those children with social, emotional, intellectual, or physical problems. If these criteria are met, preschool programs in the workplace could have a profound and positive impact on young children and their working parents.

This impact would be bound to affect the public school system. Such things as the length of the school day, the closing of schools during summer vacations and in-service training days, the arbitrary age requirement for starting school, the lack of after-school programs for latch-key children, and the ever-increasing numbers of functionally illiterate adolescents and young adults would receive closer scrutiny with an eye to change. Indeed, the corporate child-care center may precipitate a long-overdue reorganization of the entire public school delivery system.

In addition to the public schools, private child-care centers are bound to feel the effects of competition from preschool programs in the workplace. For those child-care providers who currently spend the major part of the "school" day adjusting television sets, tying unruly children to toilet seats, and watering down the colored punch served at snack time, this new school system might spell an end. The end will also be in sight for small, isolated mom-and-pop operations that lack inventive and stimulating programs — as well as for the quick-buck artists who deal in Tot Lots with any-warm-body staffing.

These changes seem likely, because local journalists are now taking a closer look at what happens to children in day care. Beginning in July 1979, for example, a two-week-long exposé, titled "The Day Care Nightmare," appeared in the *Ft. Lauderdale News*.[10] The series of articles outlined deplorable conditions that were found to exist in many of the 230 child-care facilities in Broward County, Florida. Pressure from an irate public caused the board of county commissioners to re-examine the existing child-care code. A stronger code was subsequently passed, and nine of the worst offenders dropped out of the child-care business.

Unfortunately, what occurred in Ft. Lauderdale is not atypical. The worst offenders, once exposed, do close down. But, when the smoke clears, a number of marginally acceptable child-care centers remain. And in these fewer centers, more working parents are trying to find child-care placements that will conform to their workday schedules. This situation, combined with virtual tokenism in child-care licensing standards at both the federal and the state levels, leaves large numbers of children and their families at risk. Small wonder that corporations are moving to supply child care for their employees.

Even high-quality child-care facilities are likely to feel the impact of the new corporate programs. Increased competition for enrollees, coupled with rising costs for utilities, equipment, food, and staff, will put many of these child-care centers in jeopardy. Closings will limit parental choices, but schools in the workplace will help to fill the gap.

This child-care scramble may yield one unexpected gain for educators. For the first time, we may see a formal link between two systems that have traditionally failed to communicate with one another — the public schools and the early childhood programs. Children are likely to benefit, if this link is forged.

Of course, some people will find the emergence of corporate child care threatening. Like author George Leonard, these opponents will probably express the concern that "corporations have momentum, but no heart."[11] Fear-mongers among them may play on the notion of technology and automation leading to depersonalized environments that turn out production-line people. But business and industry have a penchant for hiring the right people to do the right jobs, and this observable fact may assuage these concerns. After all, these same corporate giants brought us the pacemaker, the automobile, and even the printed word.

For now, preschool education in the workplace is at a crossroad. There is a yellow light, and we must proceed with optimistic caution.

1. *Employers and Child Care: Establishing Services at the Workplace* (Washington, D.C.: Women's Bureau, U.S. Department of Labor, 1981).

2. Ibid.

3. Mount Sinai Medical Center, *The Black Book on Child Care, 1979-82* (Miami Beach, Fla.: Department of Human Resources, January 1982).

4. Ibid.

5. Dana Friedman, *Child Care in the 80's: Reaching Out to Business and Labor* (Belmont, Mass.: Child Care Information Exchange, September/November 1980).

6. *Tax Incentives for Employer-Sponsored Day Care Programs* (Chicago: Commercial Clearinghouse, 1980).

7. *Tax Information for Divorced or Separated Individuals* (Washington, D.C.: Internal Revenue Service, Pub. No. 504); and *Credit for Child and Dependent Care Expenses* (Washington, D.C.: Internal Revenue Service, Pub. No. 2441).

8. Wanda M. Slayton, *Planning for Child Care in Dade County* (Metro-Dade County, Fla.: Department of Human Resources, 1979).

9. *CDF Reports* (Washington, D.C.: Children's Defense Fund, June 1981).

10. "The Day Care Nightmare," *Ft. Lauderdale* (Fla.) *News*, 29 July 1979.

11. George Leonard, *Education and Ecstasy* (New York: Dell, 1969).

Industry-Related Day Care: Trends and Options

Marce Verzaro-O'Brien, Denise LeBlanc, and Charles Hennon

The next decade will be characterized by an increased need for child care options in the United States (Hofferth, Moore, and Caldwell 1978; Moore and Hofferth 1979). By 1990 it is predicted there will be 23.3 million children under six, 10.4 million (about 45 percent) with working mothers (Hofferth 1979) who will need child care. As child and family advocates plan for this projected need, the specific nature of the demands which could be made on the caregiving system will have to be determined. An examination of current needs and trends is a necessary first step in the process.

CURRENT DAY CARE TRENDS

Two distinct types of caregiving systems have emerged: *individual and small group care,* which is home-based; and *group care* which is either home- or center-based. Individual care encompasses in-home care by a parent, relative, sibling, or baby-sitter, as well as out-of-home care by a sitter. Also included are family day care homes, where a caregiver has 5 or fewer children in her or his own home. Group care refers to programs for larger numbers of children, both in a home (6–12 children) and in a center (12 or more children) (Hofferth 1979). Group care can be sponsored by nonprofit and proprietary corporations, governmental agencies, and individuals.

Individual and small group care have been used more extensively than group care (Low and Spindler 1968; U.S. Bureau of the Census 1976; U.S. Department of Health, Education and Welfare 1978). In 1977, there were approximately 18,300 day care centers with an enrollment of 900,000 children (Abt Associates 1978). It must be noted however, that many working mothers depended on several types of caregiving arrangements and these change frequently (Moore and Hofferth 1979).

The data on family preferences for types of caregiving are sparse. Working mothers may perceive individual care as similar to that which their child would receive within the family (Unco 1975). However, a different preference pattern has emerged from the 1978 *Family Circle* (Women's Bureau 1979). The results, while skewed in the direction of middle- and upper-middle-class families, suggested that previous studies may have missed important child care realities. As few as 10 percent of working mothers indicated that their first preference was to leave their children with a relative, and only 20 percent now used relatives for caregiving, as opposed to 46.3 percent in 1965 (Low and Spindler 1968). Only 17.5 percent would choose individual and small group care if they could pick the arrangements they want for their children. In contrast, 44 percent would select group care, with well-trained staff and balanced and stimulating daily programs. While parents were willing to pay for group care, cost and availability remain key issues in the final selection of the type of caregiving. Thus, the historical non-utilization of group care may be a reflection of factors other than parental choice, such as the lack of available programs at a reasonable cost.

Other data also lead to the prediction of an increased need for group caregiving. Hall and Weiner (1977) demonstrated that female-headed families and small families are most likely to select group care. In the last decade, there has been an increase in the number of single-parent families, that parent most often being female (Ross and Sawhill 1975). Further, while more families will have one or two children, fewer will have three or more children (U.S. Bureau of the Census 1977). Thus, group care may be in greater demand as we move toward the 1990s.

Locating individual care providers may become increasingly difficult (Moore and Hofferth 1979). Although little is known about these people, their pay is low (Hall and Weiner 1977). Hence they may choose to enter the work force outside of their homes, or they may begin to charge more than families can pay (Schortlidge and Brito 1977). As the availability of individual care decreases, there may be a corresponding increase in the demand for group care.

Because the need for child care arrangements may well increase, so too may the demand for group caregiving escalate. What are the available means by which group care could be expanded? Discussion of options often has focused on governmental response to this perceived need. Existing programs such as Head Start, Title XX, WIN, and AFDC day care payments already provide a scattered system of governmental involvement in caregiving. In the 1970s, three national child and family service bills were proposed to provide funding for an expanded range of federally-supported child and family services, but all were defeated. The cost of such solutions as universally available, public-sponsored day care, extension of Head Start to all eligible families, and the expansion of the child care tax credit have been estimated (Congressional Budget Office 1978); but comparatively little discussion has centered on the role of labor and business in the sponsorship of group day care. If the projections of an increased need for group care are accurate, it is important to consider whether industry-related day care could be an option for that expansion.

A NEW RESPONSE TO DAY CARE?

Industry-related sponsorship of day care is not a new phenomenon. Prior to World War II, the day care involvement of business and labor was limited to health, and other scattered industries. During World War II, as more than 3 million married women entered the work force, child care became imperative. Public programs for day care were supplemented by child care programs in defense plants. The most extensive wartime day care operation was that of Kaiser Shipbuilding Corporation, who operated two centers in Portland, Oregon from November 1943 to September 1945, and served more than 4000 children. Although little has been written about these centers, their existence demonstrated that quality industry-based child care can be provided if there is a recognized need for and commitment to the task (LeBlanc and Hennon 1979).

After World War II, the interest in day care by industry and labor remained. Although descriptions of recent industry-related day care efforts are few, the Women's Bureau survey (1971) indicated that in 1970, at least eleven companies operated day care centers, with nine of them providing detailed information on their operations. Five of these companies manufactured textile products and had predominantly female work forces. The survey also found some caregiving commitment from unions (e.g., the Amalgamated Clothing Workers of America and the United Federation of Teachers), from hospitals, and from the federal government (as an employer). LeBlanc and Hennon (1979) found two of the eleven programs were still operating, but these were privately run and hence, independent of the company. All other programs had closed for these reasons: community day care filled the employee need (2); a low employee turnover led to an absence of age-eligible children (2); day care was a financial loss to the industry (1); the facility did not meet licensing regulations (1); the space was needed for business expansion (1); and unknown (2).

LeBlanc and Hennon (1979) contacted 48 other industries to ascertain their past, present, or future commitment to day care. In-depth interviews were conducted with personnel managers of 21 businesses who employed home economists—professionals who might have a commitment to children and families. None of the businesses had a day care center, nor did any of them intend to start one. Many of the personnel managers gave more than one reason for this decision. Reasons most often given were: the service was too expensive (4); no space was available (7); and the company did not claim responsibility for this type of service (9). Reasons mentioned only once included: there was a lack of employee interest, emphasis was placed on other service projects; state licensing standards are restrictive; and there was a need to retain funds for employee profit-sharing plans. In 6 businesses, employee leave was provided in order to care for a sick child, but none of these businesses provided payments for child care at other facilities.

In a comprehensive analysis of industry-related day care, Perry (1978) identified 9 day care centers sponsored by industries, 7 sponsored by the Amalgamated Clothing and Textile Workers Union, 14 sponsored by government agencies, and 75 sponsored by hospitals. The 1978 estimated enrollment in the employer-sponsored day care centers was: industry (545); labor union (1445); government agency (825); and hospital (5604). Also mentioned were facilities located on military installations. Identified by branches, the number of centers included: Army (50); Air Force (89); Navy (46); and Marine Corps (15). Estimated enrollment in military centers was 25,059 children.

Perry (1978) found differences between centers regarding years of operation, enrollment, and type of staff. Generally, military centers had been in operation the longest. Among civilian centers, hospitals had the longest history. Military-sponsored day care programs had larger enrollments than did civilian centers. The latter had more teachers with college degrees and utilized more full-time staff.

Benefits reported by 72 of the centers included the following: new employees were easier to recruit (53); absenteeism of employees was lower (49); employees developed a more positive attitude toward their work (40); employees developed a more positive attitude toward the sponsoring organization (38); and the job turnover rate of employees was lower (34).

Eighteen of the centers surveyed had closed. Reasons for this decision were: there were not enough employees wanting the service to fill the center (11); the high cost of employee subsidies (9); the center was not needed to attract and keep a steady work force (4); administrative problems (4); the facility was needed for other uses (3); and employees were unwilling to pay costs (3).

While there may have been a major effort by business and labor in the late 1960s and early 1970s to explore day care as a fringe benefit, these sectors may be phasing out their concern for the reasons highlighted above. In light of this trend, it is important for child and family advocates to decide upon the feasibility of pursuing the expansion of industry-related day care.

THE FUTURE OF INDUSTRY-RELATED DAY CARE

One approach to making this decision is to evaluate the advantages and disadvantages of industry-related day care.

Advantages

If families are to thrive, the current separation of work place from family members must be altered (Bronfenbrenner 1976). The distance between work and home prevents young children from making connections with the adult work world and deprives them of a variety of adult role models (Urban Research Corporation 1970). Child care facilities located in a parent's work place might help young children to better understand their parents' roles outside the home. Children's tours of the industry, shared lunch hours, meeting parents' co-workers and supervisors, and learning about the types of jobs performed at the parents' work place could preserve some measure of family and community integration.

Dual-career families, where both wife and husband have an equal commitment to their work, impose a unique challenge for work-family connections, especially in child care arrangements (Holmstrom 1973). These parents may have less time to spend with their young children. Availability of on-site child care could provide increased

interactions during lunch hours and the commuting time to and from work.

Industry may be undergoing important changes. For example, as increased numbers of women enter the labor force, there may be concurrent changes in worker priorities and needs. Also, Bell (1973) has suggested that America may be moving into a post-industrial society, when future economic enterprises will focus upon their socializing functions (quality of life) as well as upon their economic functions (profit making). Such changes will require creative responses from businesses and unions, one of which could be sponsored day care.

Businesses and unions both could benefit from potential decreases in worker absenteeism and tardiness which result when transient and unpredictable caregiving arrangements create daily problems for families. Stable quality child care can also reduce employee turnover. Further, a child care commitment from a business could lead to greater worker loyalty and dedication to that business. There may be tax advantages for capital expenditures with which businesses develop day care centers (Women's Bureau 1979).

Conservation of gas and other energy sources could result if parents did not have to travel extra distances to drop off and pick up their young children. Conservation of family members' time would be another important savings.

Disadvantages

Businesses may not be amenable to any pressures to include day care as a part of their commitment. In a needs assessment of 24 day care centers, Krantz, Vasquez, and Shimek (1971) found a clear consensus among businesses that, in a period of a high rate of unemployment, supportive services for employees were both unprofitable and unnecessary. Employees could be found who would neither need nor demand ancillary services such as child care. LeBlanc and Hennon (1979) found similar responses from businesses.

The day care tradition of cooperative management between parents and staff may not be as feasible in an industrial day care center. Krantz, Vasquez, and Shimek (1971) found that companies would want complete operational control of the child care services and would not seek any form of community involvement.

Unions may not see child care as a major bargaining issue when salaries, health, and retirement benefits barely keep pace with the cost of living. Only those unions with predominantly female membership may be interested in pursuing discussions of sponsored day care, because other benefits have a higher priority for many union members. The low priority given to the child care issue by unions may be particularly critical in light of the LeBlanc and Hennon (1979) finding that businesses would only consider child care benefits if they were proposed by the union.

Regardless of sponsorship, it is possible that the placing of centers near industrial areas may be detrimental to the well-being and development of young children. The increasing evidence of the negative long-term impact of industrial pollution may outweigh the value of proximity to parents' work places. Further, it may be difficult to find suitable caregiving facilities in an area zoned for industries and businesses. The costs of renovation may be prohibitive for industry.

Parents who use buses, subways, and trains to get to work may not wish to have their young children using these modes of transportation during busy hours. Also, parents may wish to spend their work breaks socializing with friends or doing home-related errands and not with their young children.

Options

Several choices are available to early childhood educators who want to become involved in industry-related child care. One role would involve serving as a resource person for both businesses who want to explore direct sponsorship of a child care program, as well as their employees. This would require knowledge of the various tax incentives available to businesses, such as the options in depreciation and amortization of child care facilities (CCH Editorial Staff 1980). Also important would be a monitoring of current Internal Revenue Service Rulings and federal tax regulations that are pertinent both to the sponsoring business and its employees.

For example, it is important that the relevant portions of the recently passed Economic Recovery Tax Act (1981) be explained, especially Section 129, which states that the gross income of an employee does not include amounts paid for or incurred by the employer for child care assistance, provided that assistance meets certain requirements described in the legislation. Further, employers will need to know that if they pay part or all of employees' child care fees, such expenses are perceived as ordinary and necessary business expenses, just as are insurance plans and other benefits. As such, all or portions of the fees are allowable as tax credits, under IRS Ruling 73-348. A similar tax credit or tax deduction may be available from various state revenue services.

A second role of child and family advocates is to work on behalf of proposed federal and state legislation that would provide additional incentives for businesses and unions to sponsor employee child care. As Goodman (1981) notes, the recent Metzenbaum-Hawkins amendment to the tax bill contained several important provisions that would have increased the tax deductions to businesses that assisted their employees in payments for child care. By advising employers and employees of pending legislation and ways to influence its passage or modification, advocates could help to ensure a more favorable climate for industry-sponsored child care.

For some businesses and unions, investment in child care facilities may be appropriate. Child and family advocates should offer their expertise to these efforts. Because the value of industry-sponsored day care is related to so many factors, creative options to direct provision of child care need to be explored. For locations where creation of centers is not feasible, other vehicles for industrial commitment are available.

Business and union leaders could serve as catalysts in conducting community-based child care needs assessments, leading to a variety of available caregiving options. Financial donations could be made to facilitate child care planning and for center start-up costs. Companies or unions could provide a staff member who assists employees in locating suitable child care. In addition, a business or union might use a voucher system, in which the employee is issued a certificate worth a specified amount toward fees for child care. The employer or union could reserve a certain number of spaces in a day care center and could contribute to the cost of care. Personnel policies could be altered to provide a greater variety of personal leaves, sabbaticals, or Flexi-time schedules, all of which would assist employees in meeting family responsibilities.

These options may well have a higher probability of success than would advocacy only for industry-sponsored day care facilities. Adopting policies such as Flexi-time, day care vouchers, and placement assistance would permit what Liljeström (1978) describes as the synchronization of family members' careers within a labor market economy. Child and family advocates should initiate contact with industry and delineate the range of available options by which business and labor can assist families to find suitable child care arrangements. Such contact may well sensitize business and union leaders to their responsibilities in maintaining family strengths, as well as to the benefits that industry can gain from its demonstration of human concern. This task presents a creative challenge for child and family advocates.

REFERENCES

Abt Associates. *National Day Care Study: Preliminary Findings and Their Implications.* Cambridge, Mass.: Abt Associates, 1978.

Bell, D. *The Coming of the Post-Industrial Society.* New York: Basic Books, 1973.

Bronfenbrenner, U. "The Roots of Alienation." In *Raising Children in Modern America,* ed. N. Talbot. Boston: Little, Brown, 1976.

CCH Editorial Staff. *Tax Incentives for Employer-Sponsored Day Care Programs.* Chicago: Commerce Clearing House, 1980.

Congressional Budget Office. *Child Care and Preschool: Options for Federal Support.* Washington, D.C.: U.S. Government Printing Office, 1978.

Economic Recovery Tax Act of 1981. *Public Law 97-34.* Washington, D.C.: United States Congress, 1981.

Goodman, E. "Public Policy Report. The Transfer-And-Pray Theory." *Young Children* 37, no. 1 (November 1981): 71–73.

Hall, A., and Weiner, S. *The Supply of Day Care Services in Denver and Seattle.* Menlo Park, Calif.: Stanford Research Institute, 1977.

Hofferth, S. L. "Day Care in the Next Decade: 1980–1990." *Journal of Marriage and the Family* 41 (1979): 649–657.

Hofferth, S. L.; Moore, K. A.; and Caldwell, S. B. *The Consequences of Age at First Childbirth: Labor Force Participation and Earnings.* Washington, D.C.: The Urban Institute, 1978.

Holmstrom, L. *The Two Career Family.* Cambridge, Mass.: Schenkman, 1973.

Krantz, M.; Vasquez, A.; and Shimek, R. *An Investigation of Local Community Needs and Resources with Reference to Twenty-Four Child Care Services.* Milwaukee, Wis.: Milwaukee Christian Center, 1971.

LeBlanc, D., and Hennon, C. B. "On-Site Child Care and Other Child Care Policies of Business Firms and Their Impact on Everyday Life." Paper presented at the annual meeting of the National Council on Family Relations. Boston, October 1979.

Liljeström, R. *Integration of Family Policy and Labor Market Policy in Sweden.* New York: Swedish Information Service, 1978.

Low, S., and Spindler, P. *Child Care Arrangements of Working Mothers in the United States.* Washington, D.C.: U.S. Government Printing Office, 1968.

Moore, K. A., and Hofferth, S. L. "Women and Their Children. In *The Subtle Revolution,* ed. R. Smith. Washington, D.C.: The Urban Institute, 1979.

Perry, K. "Survey and Analysis of Employer-Sponsored Day Care in the United States." (Doctoral dissertation, University of Wisconsin–Milwaukee, 1978).

Ross, H., and Sawhill, I. V. *Time of Transition: The Growth of Families Headed By Women.* Washington, D.C.: The Urban Institute, 1975.

Shortlidge, R. L., and Brito, P. *How Women Arrange for the Care of Their Children While They Work: A Study of Child Care Arrangements, Costs and Preferences in 1971.* Columbus, Ohio: The Center for Human Resources Research, 1977.

Unco, Inc. *National Day Care Consumer Study.* Chicago: Unco, 1975.

U.S. Bureau of the Census. *Daytime Care of Children: October 1974 and February 1975.* Current Population Reports, Series D-20, No. 298. Washington, D.C.: U.S. Government Printing Office, 1976.

U.S. Bureau of the Census. *Fertility of American Women: June 1976.* Current Population Reports, Series D-20, No. 308. Washington, D.C.: U.S. Government Printing Office, 1977.

U.S. Department of Health, Education and Welfare. *The Appropriateness of the Federal Interagency Day Care Requirements.* Washington, D.C.: U.S. Government Printing Office, 1978.

Urban Research Corporation. *Proceedings of the Conference on Industry and Day Care.* Chicago: Urban Research Corporation, 1970.

Women's Bureau. *Community Solutions for Child Care.* Washington, D.C.: National Manpower Institute, 1979.

Women's Bureau. *Day Care Services: Industry's Involvement.* Washington, D.C.: U.S. Department of Labor, 1971.

Employer-Sponsored Child Care on the Rise

By Rick Graser

U.S. and Appalachian employers are adopting revolutionary benefits packages in order to attract and retain top-notch personnel. Flexible benefits or "cafeteria plans" designed to accommodate the varied needs of employees are being implemented throughout the nation. One of the most popular of these new benefits is employer-sponsored child care services.

According to a recent publication of the Women's Bureau of the Department of Labor, the fastest-growing segment of the labor force today is mothers of preschool children. In the past decade, entrance into the labor force by these women has increased by 55 percent. Now, nearly one-half of all mothers of children under six years old either work or are looking for work.

Of paramount concern to these working mothers is the availability of reliable, quality, educationally sound child care during the workday. If working parents are not satisfied with their child care arrangements, the resulting distraction, stress and anxiety decrease productivity and increase tardiness, absenteeism, accidents and employee morale problems.

Over the years, the federal government has launched a number of programs designed to aid working parents with child care needs. Many of these programs have targeted low-income families and their children. Funds provided through Title XX of the Social Security Act, Aid to Families with Dependent Children, the Work Incentive Program, Head Start and Title I of the Elementary and Secondary Educa-

tion Act assist in providing child care to more than one million children from low-income families each year. However, the greatest portion of federal support for child care is realized through the federal income tax credit for child care. Any tax-paying parent who pays for child care in order to work or go to school may qualify for this credit.

As efforts to trim the federal budget require cuts in many of the federal child care programs, it is becoming necessary to find alternative sources of funding. Spurred by this need and the President's commitment to making quality child care available to everyone, the White House has directed several agencies to develop programs to help educate private industry on the needs and concerns of employees with child care requirements and to encourage private companies to become involved in funding and supporting child care programs.

White House Initiatives

In a pilot program, the White House Office of Private Sector Initiative sponsored three luncheons this past June at which host companies brought 20 to 30 corporate chief executive officers (CEOs) together to listen to child care professionals explain the role industry can play in providing child care services to employees. The CEOs then discussed with each other their own views and experiences with the subject. These meetings outlined for the CEOs the broad range of child care services and helped identify those particular pro-

grams that would best suit individual companies' needs.

In a questionnaire prepared by the federal sponsors and filled out by the industry participants in the programs, many of the executives expressed a real interest in investigating the many alternative types of child care programs available to industries seeking to assist employees in meeting their child care needs.

The types of family-oriented benefits and child care programs companies can provide for their employees that were described briefly to participating CEOs include:

family-oriented programs

• *flexible scheduling*—workers are allowed to choose office arrival and departure times, within certain limits, to accommodate their child care needs
• *flexible leave policies*—workers may take leave in order to attend to important family obligations, such as children's illnesses, doctor's appointments, and parent-teacher conferences or other school-related activities
• *child care information and referral services*—a company participates in a network to provide information to employees regarding available local child care to match parents' needs with those services
• *parent education programs*—companies sponsor seminars for working parents on such subjects as child development, child care and coping with conflicts between work and family
• *flexible benefit plans (so-called "cafeteria plans")*—employees may

choose from among two or more alternative benefit packages (with employees usually receiving inflexible core benefits, but being allowed to select from among alternative elective benefits such as child care services, educational assistance or even fitness programs).

child care programs

• *vendor programs*—a company issues vouchers to employees to cover all or part of their child care expenses at an existing child care center

• *charitable donations*—a company donates funds and/or services to a child care center

• *family day care systems*—employers establish a network of independent family day care providers who will supply child care services in their homes for employees' children

• *consortium center*—a group of employers work together to develop and support a child care center or program to serve their employees

• *on-site/near-site centers*—a company and/or union sponsors child care for children of employees at centers conveniently located on or near the job site.

The CEOs participating in the June luncheons registered high interest for the flexible scheduling and leave options as well as for information and referral services. They expressed somewhat less interest in charitable donations, flexible benefit plans and parent education programs, and little interest in the more costly options such as on-site/near site day care centers and the vendor/voucher programs. Federal sponsors pointed out, however, that these statistics are somewhat inconclusive because of the small sample of participants responding to the questionnaires.

The low level of enthusiasm which was generated for the on-site center option suggests that further efforts to educate industry leaders on the benefits of such in-house programs to sponsoring companies are in order. Perhaps the consortium plan should receive more emphasis as a viable alternative for small companies. Tax incentives such as capital depreciation on child care center property allowable under legislation sponsored by President Reagan and various tax-exempt programs under which an employer may establish a not-for-profit corporation to operate a center need to be stressed. And tangible corporate benefits such as increased ability to recruit among qualified job applicants with child care needs, lower absenteeism and turnover, improved employee morale, and better community relations should all be pointed out.

The success of these initial luncheons prompted the White House to schedule a number of similar functions, the first of which took place in Denver, Colorado, on September 28.

ARC Child Care Programs

The Appalachian Regional Commission (ARC) has long been active in promoting better child care services for low- and moderate-income families, and in supporting the state child care programs within Appalachia. Most recently, the Commission has sought to place more emphasis on employer-sponsored programs. ARC Federal Co-Chairman Winifred A. Pizzano comments:

Women, especially mothers of children under the age of 13, are entering the work force in record numbers. Experts tell us that this is a spiraling trend likely to continue well into the 1990s. We must recognize that public support, in tax dollars, simply cannot keep up with this increasing demand for adequate child care. That is why we must now embark on an all-out effort to encourage business and industry to become involved and to sponsor child care programs for their employees. I believe that the interests of businesses will be best served if they take the initiative now and help meet this issue head on.

The Commission has funded two important recent studies on this subject:

A project of the Winthrop College School of Consumer Science, "Family Support Systems: Alternative Child Care Arrangements" included a survey of working women, a study of employer-sponsored child care centers and the development of a multimedia marketing package to interest employers in providing child care services for their employees. The working women surveyed indicated that they would prefer child care at the work place to other types of child care arrangements.

An "Employer-Supported Child Care Study," conducted for ARC by the University Research Corporation, surveyed employer-sponsored child care programs in the United States, Appalachian child care programs, households with children enrolled in the Appalachian child care programs and Appalachian employers. Of the 228 Appalachian employers surveyed, more than 50 percent expressed an interest in learning more about employer-sponsored child care programs. The study also made recommendations for promoting employer involvement in the provision of child care services.

Over the past two years, ARC has provided seed money and technical assistance in eleven states to encourage the establishment of employer-sponsored child care services. The Commission has provided funding, or has slated future funding, for programs in Alabama, Georgia, Mississippi, New York, North Carolina, Ohio, Pennsylvania, South Carolina, Tennessee, Virginia and West Virginia.

Programs supported by the Commission have included seminars for employers, for working parents and for child care providers; efforts to help child care providers develop marketing skills and materials directed toward the business community; and studies and surveys conducted by regional universities and colleges.

New ARC Grants

Five recently approved grants stand out. The first, in North Carolina, is a comprehensive plan to revamp existing services in 25 Appalachian counties to involve industry directly in sponsoring child care programs. The second, in Mississippi, calls for training companies in 20 Appalachian counties to develop industry-supported child care facilities. The third and fourth will help fund two centers supported by hospitals in Georgia's Union and Floyd counties (Floyd Medical Center and Union General Hospital). And the fifth, in Carroll County, Georgia, funds a unique program sponsored by four companies which, together, employ approximately 1,800 women (with 400 dependent children who will benefit from the child care service provided). ARC funding is generally made available only to start up child care programs or help them with initial operating costs; they are expected to become self-supporting after one year.

In North Carolina, a state long active in the child care field, federal, state and local funds totaling $2.8 million will support a one-year transition program in 25 counties. The project will help attract industry to the area by assisting in the provision of adequate child care, will help make child care services available where job training is to be conducted in areas of critical manpower shortages and will assist industry in recruiting and retaining employees by providing child care services. This year-long program, administered by the North Carolina Department of Human Resources and sponsored by eleven local agencies, has developed a timetable to encourage private-sector involvement in the provision of child care to employees. Goals of the program include expansion of day care center boards to include in-

dustry representatives, relocation of small, inefficient centers nearer to the plants and businesses they will serve and restructuring of fee schedules to bring them closer to the true cost of providing services (but not make them greater than the market will bear). Industries with large numbers of female employees will be targeted for participation in the project. Moreover, each of the sponsoring agencies in the 25 coun-

ties has identified major activities it will initiate during the year to help achieve the overall goal of obtaining private-sector support for child care and assisting industry in maintaining a stable work force by making child care available to employees.

The Mississippi program's goals are to establish child care information and referral services in 25 industries within the area, and to establish one industry-supported day care center to serve as a model for industry-sponsored child care within Appalachian Mississippi.

The roll call of industry-sponsored on-site day care centers—which number about 600 nationally—increased during September as grants were awarded by ARC to three sponsoring groups in Georgia. The Union County Hospital Authority, citing a loss in qualified medical personnel, applied for and was granted start-up and first-year operating funds for a day care center to be located in the Union County Nursing Home. Before this grant was awarded, there were no licensed public or private child care facilities in Union County. In materials prepared for ARC, hospital and nursing home officials provided specific examples of loss of personnel and serious family/career conflicts that had been experienced by employees due to the unavailability of child care. One nurse explained that because of the prolonged illness of a family member who had previously taken care of her son, she must now travel 28 miles over mountainous terrain each day to leave her child with a back-up babysitter. Further, all of the nurses interviewed expressed concern about imposing on relatives and noted resulting strains on family relationships.

The hospital authority predicts that this new center will not only alleviate many of these problems at its two facilities but will also assist other local industries that employ large numbers of working mothers with similar child care problems. Seminars offering instruction on such topics as child health and nutrition will be offered by hospital staff to participating families. And, to the extent possible, interaction will be encouraged between nursing home residents and children at the center. Additionally, efforts will be made to involve local merchants and industry representatives in the project.

The hospital authority of Floyd

Increasing Need for Child Care			
	U.S. Women in the Labor Force	U.S. Women with Children under 6	U.S. Women in the Labor Force with Children under 6
1970	30,546,667	13,727,304	4,227,383
1980	44,740,543	13,554,175	6,211,979

Source: U.S. Bureau of the Census.

County, Georgia, echoing a need to attract and retain employees (particularly nurses), has received $128,000 from ARC to construct a day care facility at Floyd Medical Center in Rome, Georgia. The nursing staff will receive first priority in enrolling children in the program, which will initially serve two work shifts and operate between 6:30 a.m. and 12:00 midnight. The center will provide care for approximately 50 children ranging in age from six weeks to ten years.

Most of the approximately 600 employer-sponsored child care centers in the nation are operated by hospitals or other medical facilities. There appears to be a direct relationship between the interest of the health care industry in child care and the efforts of these institutions to recruit and retain qualified and experienced medical personnel, especially nurses, who are mostly women.

However, there has also been a trend toward greater involvement in the child care field within the service and manufacturing industries that have traditionally employed large numbers of women. One recent example of this trend is the successful application for ARC funding by the Bowdon Child Care Center, Inc., of Carroll County, Georgia.

The center will serve the employees—85 percent of whom are women—of four companies, the Lamar Manufacturing Company, Breman-Bowdon Investment Company, Bowdon Manufacturing Company and the Warren Sewell Clothing Company. Construction of the building that will house the center is being financed by company funds alone. And after the initial operating funds provided by the ARC grant are expended, the center is expected to operate solely on fees paid by parents and company subsidies.

The grant, which was approved on September 22, 1983, will provide $184,000—one-half of the start-up and first-year operating expenses for the Breman-Bowdon Industrial Child Care Program. The balance will be provided by the sponsoring companies. This project is the culmination of nearly five years of study and interest on the part of the four family-managed businesses that will be served by the center. L. Richard Plunkett, president of Lamar Manufacturing Company, and his father, Lamar Plunkett, have been the key negotiators and chief sponsors of the project. The companies originally became interested in providing child care for their employees about five years ago, at which time they investigated the possibility of opening a center in a large house adjacent to one of the plants. However, strict regulations and complex licensing procedures caused them to shy away from opening a center at that time. Instead, they sought the advice of people involved with the early childhood development program at West Georgia College, people who have continued to provide consulting services in the years since. These consultants informed the Plunketts of the possible availability of ARC funding, and the companies again became seriously interested in providing child care services for their employees. "We felt that as employers of working mothers in the community," explained Dick Plunkett, "we have a responsibility to try to make available resources to aid in the early development of the children of these employees." As to benefits to the companies, Mr. Plunkett says, "We hope to see lower absenteeism and expect that mothers will be less distracted from their work and feel more comfortable knowing that their children are well cared for and only a short distance away."

Although the center is not scheduled to open officially until February 1, 1984, Mr. Plunkett is optimistic that operations can begin as early as the first of the year. Describing Mr. Plunkett as a determined and forceful man, ARC staff members report that when they first visited him "with an armload of documents" to help convince him of the worth of the project, Mr. Plunkett's immediate comment was, "If it's not going to be first class, we won't do it."

Diane Hornsby, president of Georgia Child Care Providers Association, is now recruiting staff and will become the first director of the Bowdon Child Care Center. Ms. Hornsby brings several years of experience to her new post. Most recently, she served as director of the Carroll County Early Childhood Center, where she was instrumental in assisting the Breman-Bowdon group in obtaining the ARC grant. Ms. Hornsby attests to the positive attitude of the Plunketts and their organization: "When I first approached them with the proposal, they never questioned the need to provide this service for their employees—they wanted to know how to get it done." She adds, "They are a very progressive company, always interested and involved in community affairs, and truly concerned with the welfare of their employees."

"We congratulate all those involved with starting these employer-related child care programs and hope their success will inspire other business leaders to consider the advantages of sponsoring similar projects," states ARC Federal Co-Chairman Pizzano. "I believe that the positive experience thus far proves that the concept of employer-sponsored child care is sound and that these programs truly benefit everyone involved—parents, kids and employers."

Bringing Children To Work:

A Hospital Day Care Center

by Carolyn Reece

"I love it!" Nancy Adams replied when asked how she liked taking her 15-month-old daughter to work with her.

Adams is a recovery room nurse at Mount Vernon Hospital in Alexandria, Virginia, where a day care center for employees' children, aged six weeks to eight years, opened in January. A first-time mother, Adams likes "being able to drop in and see Kristina during the day. It's reassuring to see that she's being well cared for, and I can really get a 'feel' for what's going on."

The peace of mind that comes from knowing your child is nearby is high on the list of advantages parents cite for having day care available at work. Convenience is another. "I don't have to make a special trip to drop Michael off when I'm rushing to get to work," points out Mark Ziser, a pharmacist.

For employers, the provision of day care can be a plus when it comes to recruiting and retaining skilled workers. Due in part to the shortage of nurses, and to the high percentage of young women in nursing and other areas of medical work, hospitals have been in the forefront of employers offering day care. According to a study published by the Women's Bureau, more than three-quarters of the civilian employer-sponsored day care centers identified in 1978 were operated by hospitals.*

At the 5-year-old Mount Vernon Hospital, where 80 percent of the 800 employees are women of child-bearing age, the day care center offered a practical solution to meeting the needs of both employer and employees.

Like many hospitals in the area, Mount Vernon had been experiencing problems in attracting and keeping highly trained nursing and technical staff and in scheduling shifts. Early in 1980, Mount Vernon and the two other hospitals operated by the Fairfax Hospital Association discussed plans for an Association-sponsored day care facility. Because of the distances separating the hospitals, however, it was not feasible for one program to serve all three.

Later that year, an administrative resident at Mount Vernon researched various day care options—on-site care, purchasing slots for employees at a private center and using a system of satellite day care homes, for example—and did a preliminary survey to determine employees' needs. A second survey early last year revealed that the need for day care was "even more overwhelming than we had suspected, particularly for infants," said Mary Howland, director of the community relations department.

After examining the survey results and considering the options, hospital administrator Stephen Rupp backed a plan for an on-site, hospital-subsidized day care center.

"It's not inexpensive," Rupp acknowledged. Start-up costs, although modest, were about $15,000, and the hospital made a commitment to subsidize 25 to 30 percent of the costs of operating the center 12 hours a day (7:00 a.m. to 7:00 p.m.), five days a week, including breakfast, lunch and dinner, plus snacks, each day. Parents' fees were recently raised from $11.00 to $12.00 a day (prorated for those using the center less than full time), prices that are comparable to day care center rates in the northern Virginia area.

"In the long run, though," Rupp believes, "the center will help to reduce our overall costs. Job turnover and absenteeism are lower, and having the center there enhances the ability of women on maternity leave to come back to work quicker."

The center "definitely gives employees peace of mind," Rupp says—and makes for happier employees. And it's not only the employees whose children are enrolled who appreciate having the center there. Many hospital workers come in regularly just to enjoy the lively, healthy children—and supervisors need not fear that a "pool" nurse won't be available because she can't find a babysitter.

Planning for the center began last July, when Frances Damico was hired as director. Working closely with other hospital staff members, she developed a budget, established policies, met with interested parents and worked to convert a vacant 5th-floor wing into a cheerful and efficient day care center. Damico also persuaded Betty Sanborn, whom she had worked with previously, to become the new center's infant specialist.

With the start-up funds, Damico and Sanborn purchased some sturdy, versatile play equipment, cribs and infant supplies and cots for older children (supplemented by mattresses and pads from the hospital). From Sanborn's design, hospital engineers constructed movable, open room dividers from plastic piping and painted them in bright colors. The nurses' station was turned into a handy storage/work area, and a sunny area along one wall was carpeted and partially enclosed for toddlers and crawling infants.

Rooms leading from the station were set up for sleeping, reading stories and other quiet activities. One remained as a hospital room, with a bed, IV equipment, stethoscopes and other hospital supplies in it, to encourage children to role-play their parents' occupations. A nurses' lounge became the Parents' Place, where parents and staff members can relax and talk, or browse through materials on infant care and child development.

Flexibility in programming was an important consideration, since the center had to accommodate a wide age range of children who come and go throughout the day depending upon their parents' schedules, or who attend only two or three days a week if their parents work part time.

That the center operates so

smoothly, with no noticeable disruption to ongoing activities, Damico attributes to her staff: experienced and well-trained caregivers who are committed to her goals of providing support to families and enriching social, physical and intellectual experiences for even the youngest of children. The 10 permanent staff members—four of whom hold master's degrees in early childhood education—are supplemented by adult and teenage volunteers, arranged through the hospital's volunteer office.

In fact, it's the "warmth," "love," "caring" and "individual attention" that parents cite first as the center's most important and satisfying aspects. "It's much more than baby care," says Ziser, who has noticed a "marked improvement" in 2½-year-old Michael's socialization skills since he began attending a few months ago.

Nancy Adams, who currently uses the center only one or two days a week until she returns to work full time, is impressed that caregivers remember Kristina's daily routine and can ease her comfortably into the center's. Harriet Hoben, a medical transcriptionist who works the 3:00 to 11:00 p.m. shift, is happy that Danny, a 1st-grader and one of the oldest children enrolled, has an opportunity to assume a helping role with staff members and the younger children.

One of the most popular features with parents are the written reports staff members send home every day, capsuling the highlights of each child's day. Infants' feeding and changing times are given, and narratives point out social and developmental milestones the children are attaining—"It looks like Jason is about ready to walk," for example.

Currently, the center enrolls 94 children of 74 employees. So far, there have been few requests to extend the hours of daily operation or to keep the center open on weekends. Should there be a demand, however, Damico will try to accommodate parents.

There is also the unresolved problem of transporting children who need after-school care from their schools to the day care center. Hoben manages by bringing Danny and Ricky, who is in kindergarten, with her when she reports to work at 3:00—and either her husband or 18-year-old son are available to pick them up when they finish work. The hospital is investigating after-school and expansion possibilities with some of its neighbors, including a community mental health center and medical and professional office buildings.

Damico believes that employers have a "moral obligation" to see that children are cared for. "If employers cannot afford to operate a facility, they can at least offer space and let the center pay for itself," she points out. "The time has passed when parents have a choice about working, and hospitals, in particular, should have a commitment to helping children and families."

The support, interest and commitment to the center from all departments of the hospital have been, Damico says, "outstanding." And, she notes, "We don't have 'parent relationship' problems. The center is right here—we encourage parents to come in and see their children and what we do with them. There's a feeling that we're all part of the same Mount Vernon Hospital family." ■

*Kathryn Senn Perry, *Child Care Centers Sponsored by Employers and Labor Unions in the United States,* Women's Bureau, U.S. Department of Labor, 1980.

Child Care At Conferences: A Family Approach

by Julie Carvalho

On a veranda of the Washington Hilton, Gary, Randy and Michael splashed themselves and their surroundings with water from a water play table. The boys, aged 9 to 12, seemed oblivious to the sweltering August heat or the newness of their friendships. Behind the sliding doors, several younger children were sitting around child-size tables with a teacher, engrossed in art, puzzles and a typewriter. Next door, five toddlers were deciding whether to doze off on their mats, while three infants were asleep in cribs and four were being fed, changed or amused by nurses.

After several years' discussion and a year's planning by Federally Employed Women (F.E.W.), a child care space for our 1980 national training conference had become a reality.

Using various arrangements, a growing number of national organizations are providing child care at conference sites. Organizations have found that they can attract more parents, including more single parents and members of minority groups, if child care is available during meetings. One advantage of this increased participation is that the nature of discussion on human issues may broaden if people who are not "childfree" contribute their perspective.

In such human service organizations as the American Psychological Association (APA), both parents may be members and wish to bring their children with them if high quality child care is provided. Parents have reported that they can enjoy the meetings without undue worry, expense or strain. With child care available, more women can enter traditionally male fields where frequent out-of-town meetings are required.

Children can learn from the travel and meetings, be near their parents and meet children in similar situations—advantages that hotel "baby-sitting" referrals can't match. Adelle Cox Convention Services and Consultants, Inc., which runs children's hospitality centers for APA and other organizations, has cared for some of the same children from infancy through their adolescent years, as their parents attended annual conferences in different cities. With such continuity, children may look forward to seeing the same staff and youngsters again.[1] Hotels, too, may prefer such family-oriented conferences, one hotel convention director asserts.

As successful as many sites have been, others have foundered because they did not consider the ways in which child care at conferences differs from conventional child care. For example, the children who come to these centers may be weary from plane or car trips. They are exposed to strange people and surroundings, with no gradual introduction permitted. Center staff members do not have time to become familiar with a child's personality and habits over a few months; they must adjust to dozens of new children immediately. In addition, parents and children may have erratic schedules, including evening sessions for parents and odd meal hours. Some parents may also have special expectations for this kind of child care—one mother was disappointed with a conference center evening program for older children of movies, stories and simple food; she had expected a tour of the hotel and gourmet dishes for her youngsters.

Once a conference is planned, the organization must determine whether there is enough interest in and need for child care among the members. If so, the center program should be publicized early; families who might bring their children often need several months' lead time and budgeting to decide whether and how to arrange it.

Costs

The organization must decide how much of the cost it is willing to share. It might pick up the whole cost, subsidize part of it, or offer the care at cost, in which case payments could be made according to a flat fixed fee or an hourly rate. If a center attracts even 20 parents who might not otherwise attend the conference and they fill vacancies in workshops, their registration fees can help pay for the site. Because infant care is very expensive and there are other opportunities for adolescents, an organization may decide to limit the ages of eligible children at either end of the age scale. In any case, a genuine commitment to providing professional child care is needed before any decision to offer such care is made. Provision of care at a conference does open an organization to some risk. And from an attending family's point of view, a center promised but then unavailable can result in changed plans, at best, or makeshift care at worst.

Depending upon the features an organization chooses to include in its child care center, the cost per child will probably range from $5.00 to $15.00 per day.

Planning

A workplan and tentative budget must be developed early as part of the conference planning. Information obtained from early registrants on age and other characteristics of the children to be enrolled, and the length of time they will be in the center, forms the basis for many of the decisions needed. The organization should decide in advance whether the center site will be able to accommodate all the children who show up, only those who have been preregistered, or a limited number of late registrants as well, on a space-available basis.

The organization should appoint a committee chairperson or co-chairpersons with a demonstrated interest and background in child care—and with no other responsibilities for the conference. Enlisting the services of a consultant with specialized experience in arranging child care sites may be a useful investment to avoid any waste of time and funds. Our consultant, Carol Rudolph, was able to identify many resources for us and to anticipate needs that even a teacher or parent might not.[2]

Location

Early in the planning, a child development specialist should visit possible sites to decide on those most appropriate. The organization may assign the committee space at one of its hotels, or the committee can negotiate with the hotel's convention staff for suitable space and equipment. However, some hotels may back off at this point because they are not familiar with child care centers or consider them too much trouble. After we had had a series of disappointments regarding arrangements made with the hotel we had announced for the F.E.W. site—and an increasing number of infants had been registered for attendance—we switched to another hotel. It was less conveniently located but its staff was interested in housing a family activity and offered us groundfloor rooms suitable for use with the babies and other children.

Other sites to consider are local child care centers, with whom the organization or individual parents may arrange for child care. However, most centers close around 6 p.m., a factor which would limit parents' conference participation.

Insurance

Insurance can be arranged with the carrier for the organization, the conference or the hotel, or it can be arranged independently, which is far more expensive. Parents may need to sign statements absolving the organization and hotel from responsibility (assuming that reasonable care is given) if insurance is to be obtained at an affordable cost. The carrier may stipulate center location, caregiver-child ratios and other requirements in order to underwrite a group site. Local ordinances do not usually affect the operation of short-term centers, but their requirements should be checked.

Center Activities

After the committee has determined the ages and other characteristics of children likely to attend the child care center, it can develop a schedule of activities. Because the children may initially be tired, there should be flexible provision for rest and quiet activities. Enough space for children to exercise is also needed.

Field trips for older children should be coordinated with a local resident familiar with local transportation and the other logistics of moving children safely.

In 1981, the F.E.W. conference in Indianapolis featured a chartered bus trip to the zoo, a public bus trip to the Indianapolis Children's Museum, and walks to historic areas near the conference. Videotapes of programs for children were also available on-site for children who wished to stay at the center.

A separate quiet room at the child care center is useful so that energetic youngsters do not keep the tired ones awake. Depending on the distribution of children and their own inclinations, center planners may want to separate children by age groups or encourage some mingling, with older ones caring for the younger ones. Faced with 1,000 children for an evening, while attendees at an insurance conference listened to an address by the president, Adelle Cox set up separate theme parties for each of several age groups among the children.

Staff

Probably the largest portion of the center budget will be used to pay center staff members. The staff should consist of professionals whose training is appropriate to the ages of the children enrolled. A contingent of persons available on-call should also be arranged for—if the number of children attending is larger than anticipated or in case some staff members don't show.

Volunteers, including the elderly, teenagers and older children, can fill gaps if they are properly briefed and supervised. The F.E.W. program in Washington, D.C. relied on a nursing agency and several teachers, teenagers, and F.E.W. volunteers to staff the child care center. We were unsuccessful in interesting local volunteer agencies, schools or conference participants to donate a few hours, even with the offer of a certificate or free workshops. Since a large percentage of volunteers do not show in such an activity, a program should not count on them in planning the staff/child ratio.

The Indianapolis F.E.W. child care center drew staff members from a local day care center and from relatives of committee members who were skilled with children. (Some of them were men.) To find appropriate child care workers, Adelle Cox asks a registered nurse to select nurses from a children's hospital or similar institution in the convention city.

In selecting center staff members, the child care committee should look for a professional who will take the initiative in playing with small children, rather than one who will just check the children physically, as some nurses used to home assignments have done at conference sites.

Some hotels have lists of bonded "sitters" who could be checked for use as back-up workers.

An organization may urge the use of nonprofessionals as the basic staff to reduce costs. One organization official told me that "Mothers don't have to be registered nurses or certified teachers before they have children." I responded that the needs of children in an "instant center" are very special, while parents have time to get to know their children—usually one at a time. Cutting costs on staff may be counterproductive if it results in poor care which jeopardizes the children's health and safety—and the organization's reputation. Experienced, skilled parents and professionals can best handle an emergency with sketchy information on a child, or discover the cause of a strange child's distress. On the other hand, good staff members can help save expenses, by their ability to use simple materials for games and projects, for example.

Safety and Health

If an organization is lucky, the worst that happens is that a child drinks the left-over coffee of a careless staff member. On the other hand, it may care for a child who has an epileptic seizure even though the parent had not indicated the child was susceptible. As in other child care, a trained child care staff and preparation for possible emergencies are the keys in avoiding disaster.

An organization may decide to have parents bring records of their children's shots, fill out a physical examination form and sign a medical release. Or it could ask the parents to answer some basic questions, certify their child's current health and sign a release.

Any medication to be given a child should be handled with the same procedures a regular center would use, but more concern for identifying each child and his or her supplies, of course, will be needed. All instructions from children's medical records should be posted, along with emergency procedures and verified phone numbers. Each staff member should be given a copy of the center's operations schedule and other information they can refer to. For our center, we asked a consultant to provide written information on how to handle children's feelings about separation in the center.

A "No Smoking" rule may need enforcement, especially with volunteers who feel they can do as they wish since they're not being paid.

Written agreements on first aid procedures, any back-up activities of the hotel and use of local emergency rooms will be necessary. The insurance company and the hotel may have instructions to give on evacuation—a drill with the chief center staff members for each period is advisable. Special procedures may also need to be planned for any walks or trips to be taken by the children. Because you won't know the children's habits, it is more important than usual to have assignments for hand-holding and head-counting.

Depending on the location of the center, some monitoring devices for the children will be needed. Adelle Cox requires a sign-in and sign-out procedure before a child can enter or leave the center, and parents' signatures are compared with those on the registration forms. The firm also posts monitors in the halls to prevent children from wandering away or strangers from entering.

Schedules for parents and children should also be readily available at the center.

Some parents may resist the forms and procedures, on the grounds that they will not be separated from their children for long periods. However, this is one area that requires co-operation. For instance, after reading the remarks of parents who preregistered, our consultant and I were able to identify each of the children as they began playing. Because we knew something about them—whether they were timid or aggressive, for example, we could head off some problems and deal with others. In one case, we asked several staff members to console a toddler known to "want his mummy"; when his mother returned, he pointed to the large woman who had been successful and said, "Mummy, I want *that*."

Food

For our conference, we solicited and received vouchers from local food stores to help develop a low-budget but nutritious menu. Every hour and a half, to cover each of the children entering or leaving, we served a nutritious meal or snack. Only one child was known to have overindulged—most of them were too busy with activities.

Because the temperature had hit 103° in Washington, D.C. that week, we avoided bringing in milk and felt that even the hotel milk might not sit well with kids. Lemonade and less spoilable finger foods were avidly eaten each day. A home casserole was brought in frozen and warmed on a separate burner we'd bought. Mothers of infants were asked to bring and prepare their children's bottles.

If preparing food at the center is difficult, parents can be asked to bring in food for their child. Or the organization can contract with the hotel for meals or purchase food from local restaurants or order room service—in order of increasing expense. Whatever procedure is used, a method for reminding staff members of children's allergies and special food needs is necessary.

Equipment and Supplies

The hotel is the first source of such equipment as refrigerators and cribs, and of such supplies as linens, since there's no problem with delivery. At our meetings, the children enjoyed using such conference equipment as overhead projectors, movie projectors and tape recorders; but the machines had to be reserved and funds allotted for them weeks ahead.

The local Convention Bureau or Chamber of Commerce may have sources for renting cribs, playpens and feeding chairs. Some rental services will deliver and pick up items, and supply more when needed. Local child care or church facilities may also lend equipment and toys, but the time and transportation involved in dealing with them may exceed the cost of renting. We used the public library to borrow movies, records and books for the center. (We had to replace a few taken home by the children.) Videotape playback machines and cassettes can be rented for a week or weekend, or a parent may oblige.

In Washington, D.C., we obtained specialized furniture and toys from a clinic at nearby Georgetown University Hospital. Children's supply firms may also send equipment on consignment for sale to parents or local centers after the conference; one corporation sent us several boxes of toys and mats which were eagerly bought afterwards. Step-stools and potty seat converters were brought by us for each of the bathrooms.

If an organization plans to have child care centers at several conferences, it may wish to invest in permanent equipment or toys, which could be transported to each conference city.

Publicity and Preregistration

The first link in the chain is adequate notice to parents who may wish to use the child care center. Enough information should be provided to enable parents to make a decision in advance. Preregistration of at least some of the children gives the staff some idea of the characteristics of the group and the personalities of individual children. Sufficient lead time is necessary to have initial notices on the center included in the mailing of conference materials. Later, a separate mailing to parents requesting information is less likely to get lost in the shuffle of papers.

Parents' Roles

Parents' responses to the center, whether they're paying for the child care or not, will range from offers to help to resistance in providing information and supplies for their child. During one of our conferences, one mother volunteered to spell the director during the long evening. In contrast, another had to be tracked down to provide basic information on her child. A third mother brought equipment and toys to be shared at the center, while another sent her children over in a cab with no information about them except that provided by the oldest, a 12-year-old.

As in routine child care, frequent interchanges with parents prevent major problems. We sent parents a welcoming letter, specific center information and news of any changes in plans. The staff could accommodate the reasonable requests of some parents but insisted that others abide by the rule to prepare their own infant's bottles.

If any slip-up occurs, acknowledging it to the parent should ease the situation.

Providing information on children was one of our goals for our conference child care center. To decorate the walls, we hung International Year of the Child posters. A group of books on childrearing and booklets on parents' resources were available in a parents' corner.

A conference child care center also offers an opportunity for guidance to parents seeking it. At one site, a father who had long been puzzled by his son's behavior was told that we had noticed several symptoms of hyperactivity and we suggested that he discuss this with his pediatrician.

We included our recommendations on local trips for children in one of our mailings and the conference magazine also had an extensive listing of them. However, we urged parents to spend some time each day with their children rather than just arrange tours for them. (A treat for my daughters in Indianapolis was a luncheon where Congresswoman Shirley Chisholm spoke, while my son enjoyed a song fest.)

Evaluation and Replanning

Parents were candid in reporting what they liked or disliked about features of our center. (Fortunately, more of the former was reported.) Open-ended questions sought specific information on how parents and children had felt about the center before, during and after the conference.

We also discovered we had learned a surprising amount about each child in a few days and we conveyed to the parents our enjoyment of their children.

We held a briefing session with our chief child care staff members to decide what we would do differently next time and we prepared a set of recommendations for the conference board. The detailed expense vouchers we had were useful in budgeting for the next conference. The best formal evaluation procedures, however, may not be as useful as the observations of parents and children. When one 6-year-old visiting the engaging Air and Space Museum told her father she'd rather come back to the F.E.W. center "to play games again with my new friend," we knew we had achieved success.[3]

Recommendations

It is likely that more children will be accompanying their parents during conference meetings and other adult activities in the coming years. Child development professionals can help this be a source of growth for those involved. Based on the experiences of several organizations which have attempted child care at conferences and training sessions, seven recommendations have emerged:

● The organization must have a firm commitment to quality child care and, once the center is announced, help the child care committee overcome problems and obstacles.

● The committee responsible for operating the child care center needs to have specialized expertise in group child care.

● Child care should be made part of the conference plans from the outset and its availability publicized early.

● The director of the child care center must clarify expectations of the parents, organization, staff and hotel, and he or she should provide information to insure understanding of the actual arrangements.

● Before the conference, the director should obtain as much information as possible on the children to be enrolled, insure parents' cooperation when needed and, when appropriate, provide feedback to parents.

● A mix of nurses, teachers and other professionals should staff the center. Gaps in staffing can be filled by volunteers of various ages and backgrounds. Both groups of caretakers should be briefed before the conference.

● The committee should establish stringent requirements to maintain quality care and it should develop back-up resources for all arrangements.

As my 12-year-old son and I were lugging heavy equipment to the Hilton Hotel in the heat of the July F.E.W. meeting, we asked each other whether this level of work was needed for child care. The next year, as I watched a parent remove an overstimulated youngster from a conference activity, I wondered whether this new social movement was helpful. But then, as the children were leaving, I heard them talk about the men, women and children they'd met, and the places they'd enjoyed with their parents. And when I heard them ask their parents, "Can we go with you next year?" I knew I had the answer.   ■

[1]Adelle Cox, Convention Services and Consultants, Inc., 321 N.W. 186th Street, Miami, Fla. 33169.

[2]Carol Rudolph, Child Care Management Resources, 5620 Greentree Road, Bethesda, Md. 20817.

[3]Copies of forms, correspondence and other materials used in the planning and operation of the 1980 F.E.W. child care center are available at $2.00 (for the cost of duplication and mailing) from Julie Carvalho, 11668 Mediterranean Court, Reston, Va. 22090.

Section IV:
Parental Concerns

Introduction

This final group of articles focuses upon specific issues of concern to everyone connected with day care, but especially to parents. The vast majority of parents are deeply concerned about the physical and emotional well-being of their children. The desire or necessity for both parents (or the single parent) to work places a great burden on them to find what they believe will be a safe and caring environment for their children. One only has to listen to news broadcasts or read a newspaper, however, to know that occasionally even well-meaning parents have unknowingly entrusted their children to irresponsible individuals who have allowed serious injustices to occur.

Candace E. Trunzo reiterates these same concerns in her article "The ABC's of Selecting a Day-Care Center," but also includes comments from professionals regarding what are generally considered to be beneficial aspects of center-based care. To assist parents in making informed day care choices, Trunzo has compiled a list of questions that should be posed to day care personnel or answered as a result of a personal visit. Comments are provided with each question as a basis for evaluating the answer given or observed.

Also addressing the difficult job of selecting appropriate care is Peggy Patten's article, "How to Choose the Best Day-Care Program for Your Child." Again, a question-answer format is used to specify areas to which the parent should pay particular attention. Questions are listed under the headings of curriculum, staff, physical space, and family-school relations.

While these first 2 articles focus primarily on center-based care, "Including Parents in Evaluating Family Day Care Homes" examines the family day care setting and the involvement of parents in family day care regulation. While most family day care homes operate under some type of standards, parents are often not informed as to what these standards are. Mary Winget, W. Gary Winget, and J. Frank Popplewell report on a study of parents using family day care who were asked to share in

the evaluation of the homes they used. The most prevalent concerns of parents are discussed, and the greatest deficiencies found are detailed.

The final 3 articles in this section deal with health and safety concerns of parents using some form of day care for their children. Earline D. Kendall, in "Child Care and Disease: What Is the Link?," discusses recent research on illnesses of children in day care settings and whether or not they are more prevalent among these children than for children cared for in family homes. Three illnesses are highlighted: hepatitis, diarrheal diseases, and influenza type B (H-flu). The article concludes with a list of practical suggestions for care providers to help decrease the spread of disease.

Susan S. Aronson's "Injuries in Child Care" provides knowledge about the source of injuries in a day care environment. Aronson lists indoor and outdoor equipment associated with injuries to children in day care settings by frequency from a study using insurance claims. Suggestions are given for preventive measures that may help to reduce potential problems.

Child sexual abuse is, unfortunately, a topic that has recently been associated with day care settings. While the vast majority of abuse cases occur in the home, the fact that it can and has happened in child care settings makes it a matter of great concern to parents and child care providers alike. In "The Sexual Abuse Issue: How Can Child Care Providers Respond?," several child care professionals discuss such concerns as the impact of this problem on parents and providers; approaches to dealing with the media; regulatory remedies; supervisory responsibility; staff, parent, and child education; and ways to reassure parents. The last portion of the article contains an annotated list of books on sexual abuse of children as well as the names and addresses of regional resource centers that provide information, consulting, and training services.

The ABCs of Selecting a Day-Care Center

Here's a checklist of questions to ask before you enroll your kids.

by Candace E. Trunzo

ike many women who work, Kansas City accountant Joyce Emery, 33, had mixed emotions about returning to the office in 1982 after 2½ years as a full-time mother to her two daughters—Brooke, now 6, and Lindsey, 3. Says she: "I felt my kids needed home care. But I feared I'd fall behind in my career." Emery and husband Donald, 35, a corporate labor-relations negotiator, compromised by paying a neighborhood woman to look after the girls at her house. But the babysitter provided only perfunctory care and complained whenever the couple couldn't collect them by 6 p.m. Recalls Joyce: "I began to feel guilty about my decision to go back to work."

Last fall the Emerys decided to search for day care more in sync with the demands of their careers and with their children's learning curves. After inquiries at four preschools, they enrolled the girls in La Petite Academy, a Kansas City-based commercial chain with 23 local branches and a total of 380 outlets nationwide. La Petite isn't small; Brooke and Lindsey share weekdays with about a hundred kids, aged six weeks to six years. But the Emery *jeunes filles* were quickly sold on La Petite's curriculum, which ranges from computer-aided language and math lessons to field trips to watch pizza chefs at work. And the center's monthly tuition—$380 for two children—is only $20 more than the babysitter's bill.

Every working parent should be so lucky. While the growing needs of two-career families have fostered many more day-care options, selecting the one that's best suited to your budget and your kids' upbringing isn't child's play. Many couples no longer can count on the tradi-tional child-care solution—grandmother or another female relative—or afford a nanny. Nursemaids who work 45-hour weeks typically command $900 or more per month, exclusive of employer-paid vacations and Social Security taxes.

s a result, nearly 20% of working mothers must choose among competing types of group care— sole proprietorships, non-profits, cooperatives and commercial chains—that vary widely in terms of their size, staff qualifications and requirements for state licenses. Although such licenses help to ensure that day-care facilities meet minimum health, fire-safety and staffing standards, they offer no assurances that a center has been vetted as a safe haven from incompetents— or worse. The much publicized trial of teachers at the Virginia McMartin pre-school in Manhattan Beach, Calif. involves 115 charges of child pornography and sexual molestation at a state-licensed center. It was owned by a congenial grandmother who was respected in this affluent Los Angeles County community.

Though unsettling, reported incidences of day-care-related neglect or physical abuse of children remain relatively rare, says Vivian Weinstein, a professor of pediatrics at Los Angeles' King Drew Medical Center. Her staff found that only eight of 661 child-abuse cases reported during a recent nine-month period could be traced to day-care centers or elementary schools.

Bear in mind that most group-care providers are unregulated. Licenses are held by only 10% of the estimated 1.4 million homes, usually run by women, that take in two to six children per staff member. The remainder of these homes are informal operations that aren't subject to—or don't bother with—state requirements. In addition, there are around 20,000 licensed day-care centers that each look after between 50 and 200 kids. About half of these are nonprofit centers sponsored by churches, universities, cooperatives and companies as a service to employees. The rest are commercial ventures ranging from independents to major chains such as La Petite Academy, Kinder-Care and Children's World.

roup day care is still an issue of controversy among specialists in the field of child development. But government studies suggest that pre-schoolers generally benefit from such care, notes Allen Smith, a spokesman for the Department of Health and Human Services. Says he: "Day-care children tend to be more social, assertive and verbally advanced than kids of comparable ages raised at home." Counsels Harvard pediatrician T. Berry Brazelton: "Even infants thrive in centers where each one is played with sensitively."

The cost of group care depends largely on two factors: a child's age and the number and experience of the attending staff. The Department of Health and Human Services found that monthly fees for infants under age two averaged $280 nationally, compared with $240 for children three years or older. Day-care homes and employer-sponsored programs are usually less expensive than the national average. Centers that place their charges in small groups tended by specially trained teachers can be considerably more. At Houston's Montessori Country Day School, where 80% of the staff have degrees in early childhood education, monthly tuition is $450 for infants and $325 for children aged three to five. The center employs one teacher for every three youngsters under age three—or for

Uncle Sam helps to defray the cost of day care with a tax credit for working couples and single parents.

every eight preschoolers.

Uncle Sam helps to defray the cost of day care with a tax credit for working couples and single parents. Example: If your annual family income is $28,000 or higher, your credit is equal to 20% of your yearly child-care expenses, up to $2,400 for one dependent and $4,800 for two or more. That's a tax reduction of up to $480—or $960—a year.

The principal advantages of large day-care centers over intimate home-based proprietorships are greater flexibility of hours and broader curriculums. Chains and commercial centers typically have more modern facilities than nonprofit providers, many of which operate in church basements. But nonprofits often allocate a larger percentage of their budgets to salaries to attract better trained teachers and reduce staff turnover—a problem at some chains that pay minimum wages. Couples who have time to get involved may want to consider joining a cooperative. A co-op's primary attraction isn't cost savings but control: parents constitute the board of directors, hire teachers and manage finances. But they must also donate several hours a month to activities such as fixing seesaws and cleaning classrooms.

o help you better assess the group-care options in your neighborhood, *Money* has compiled the following checklist of questions to pose to providers and fellow parents before you enroll your children:

▶ How large are groups or classes at the center? According to the government-sponsored National Day Care Study published in 1979, big groups tend to be too confusing for babies and toddlers. The maximum number of infants under two years should be eight per group, while toddlers aged two to three shouldn't be placed in groups larger than 12.

▶ What is the ratio of staff to children? This is especially important for infants, who need constant cuddling and attention. There should be at least one adult for every three or four babies or every six toddlers, advises Gwen Morgan, a professor of early childhood education at Wheelock College in Boston.

▶ Are teachers readily accessible? Most centers encourage parents to drop by anytime for a chat (be wary of those that don't). And formal conferences to evaluate a youngster's progress should be scheduled at least twice a year.

▶ Is there a wide variety of toys designed to appeal to your child's age group? Infants like colorful mobiles, mirrors and plastic boxes. Toddlers' short attention spans demand lots of books, puzzles and modeling clay. With preschoolers, look for musical instruments, games and costumes as well as slides and swings.

▶ Does the center offer a reasonable mix of organized and free play? Group activities often make children "people weary," explains Gwen Morgan. There should be scheduled intervals in which kids can unwind with, say, a coloring book. If youngsters are wandering about aimlessly, however, you have to wonder how attentive teachers are.

▶ What kind of food is served? If your child has been raised on homemade soups and whole-grain breads, you should try to find a center that provides such healthy fare. Make sure kids receive ample servings and can ask for second helpings.

Name tags on bottles and toothbrushes reduce mix-ups.

▶ Are teachers conscientious about sanitary conditions? Kids under age three in day care contract about 30% more gastrointestinal ailments such as diarrhea than those who stay at home, warns Larry Pickering, a professor of pediatrics at the University of Texas Medical School in Houston. Note whether employees wash their hands before and after changing diapers or feeding babies. There should be name tags on bottles and toothbrushes to reduce mix-ups.

▶ Have arrangements been made for medical emergencies? A nurse or doctor should be available nearby, if not on call. Parents should be informed promptly when there are outbreaks of illnesses such as chicken pox or measles.

▶ Are the names of parents freely given as references? Get in touch with several and ask them some of these questions. You should also double-check the center's reputation with your local departments of health and social services.

Once you've settled on a day-care center, continue to monitor it for changes in programs or personnel. Your child's enthusiasm may be your best indicator. If the little dear sideswipes you as you try to kiss him or her good-bye at the center's door, chances are you made the right choice.

How to choose the best day-care program for your child

by Peggy Patten

Day-care centers and programs vary as much as the families that use them. As parents you want to feel that you have chosen the best day-care program for your child.

Two good ways to judge the quality of a center are to talk with parents whose children attend the center and to visit the center. When you visit a center, you can observe its program firsthand and talk with the administrative or program director. You can learn much by observing an activity period, a group time, or even a snack, bathroom, or rest time.

The selection of a day-care center for your child of course will be based on center location, cost, and number of hours open. More importantly four major concerns when making your evaluation are the following:

- curriculum
- staff
- physical space
- family-school relations.

Curriculum

What is the center's philosophy of early childhood education? Ask the director to define the center's educational goals. Staff should recognize that children learn in different ways and at different rates. A good center values children's learning through inquiry and active involvement and considers a child's physical, emotional, social, creative, and cognitive development. Emphasis should be placed on the process of learning how to think rather than learning what to think.

- Is there a planned daily program? Is it based on both short-term (daily) and long-term (weekly, monthly) goals?

Ask the director to go over the daily schedule with you. If there is a planned weekly program and units of study planned on a longer basis, ask to have these described.

- Does the center's planned program promote learning? A balance is needed between vigorous play and quiet play; indoor and outdoor activity; large-group, small-group, and independent involvement; and teacher-directed and child-directed experiences. The program should ask for input from children and consider their interests.

A wide range of activities should be offered, both in content of activity, spanning a number of curricular and developmental areas, and also in range of difficulty. Are children given choices when selecting activities? Is independence encouraged?

Note the noise level in the classroom. Is it at a healthy level that indicates productive involvement? Are children using materials freely and with respect? Ask the director if there are opportunities for a variety of experiences such as taking field trips and having visitors. Is there sufficient rest time and is it a satisfying experience with enough adults present? Are meals and snacks nutritious and varied and spaced appropriately throughout the day?

- Is there evidence of good relationships among children? Children should be encouraged to respect other children's needs. Conflicts need to be avoided by effective scheduling, physical space arrangement, availability of materials, and clear guidelines for classroom behavior. When conflicts do arise between children, how are they resolved? Are children given some responsibility in resolving their conflicts, and are they given effective strategies for doing so? Are conflicts resolved effectively and in a way that makes sense to children?

Staff

Does the center meet your state's minimum requirements for group size and teacher-child ratio in early childhood education?

- Ask the director about the training and experience of the staff.
- Do all teachers meet at least the minimum requirements for teacher training in early childhood education in your state?

To find out your state's requirements you can ask the center's administrative director; call your regional licensing office; or ask your local library's reference librarian for a copy of current licensing standards or where the regulating agency in your area is located.

Do staff members meet regularly to discuss and evaluate program goals? Do staff members strive to continue their professional growth and development by attending workshops, seminars, conferences, and classes?

- Is there evidence of good teacher-child relationships? Mutual caring and respect between teachers and children can be judged by the tone and content of their interactions. Note whether teachers interact often with children and whether children freely approach the staff. Interactions should not consist primarily of corrections and reminders, but should be concerned more with children's interests, involvement, and ideas. Guidance techniques need to be fair, consistent, and clear to children. Do staff members promote healthy self-concepts in children by maintaining high, but fair, expectations for each child by discussing feelings, and by encouraging children to exchange ideas and beliefs?

Physical space

Is the environment large enough to accommodate a variety of activities and equipment? Although requirements vary from state to state, common minimums are at least 35 square feet of usable floor space per child indoors and 75 square feet of play space outdoors. Is there enough space so that adults can walk between sleeping children's cots?

- Does the facility take into account a child's health and safety? The facility should have good light, heat, and ventilation, and should be clean. Equipment and materials need to be in good repair, with proper cushioning in areas with swings, climbers, and slides. Are sinks and toilets clean and accessible to children and adults? Are toxic substances safely stored?

Each child should have an individual cot or mat, and there should be a place provided in case a child is ill and needs

Family-school relations

Does staff acknowledge and respect family cultural backgrounds and lifestyles? Efforts should be made to become aware of family matters that may affect the child.

■ Does the center value family involvement? Find out how parents are involved in the program and how they are informed of their child's activities and progress in the program. Are families encouraged to visit and observe the center and participate in the program?

■ Is the center staff knowledgeable about community resources and professional agencies? Does staff share information with families about opportunities and services available?

Keep these criteria in mind when you observe the center and when you ask questions of the center director or parent involved in the program. While this checklist will help you in your evaluation, don't overlook the value of your own common sense when making your decision.

Day-care centers are busy places. Be sure to call in advance to make an appointment to speak with the director or to observe the program. Some centers may have printed information to give to parents, while other centers may prefer to pass along information in person. In either case, the information is available to interested parents.

Educate yourself. If a visit can only be a half hour at lunch, at the beginning or end of the day, it will be worthwhile. If you only have time for a phone call and it is a busy time at the center, ask when a good time would be to call again and discuss the program over the phone.

The benefits of a good day-care experience extend throughout your child's life. Your decision should be an informed one.

How good is your child's day care?

If your child is enrolled in a day-care program, make sure that the quality of that program is as good as you think it is. The price alone is no guarantee of quality.

These are some conclusions suggested by a study of 30 Dallas-area day-care programs made by Deborah Lowe Vandell, a University of Texas at Dallas psychology professor, as reported in the November 29 *Report on Preschool Programs* newsletter.

Vandell found that the day-care programs overall were meeting a low-quality standard of care. She attributed this mainly to the fact that Texas has the lowest day-care standards in the nation, requiring only that day-care workers be 18 years old and healthy.

Describing the situation in Dallas as "grim," Vandell said that even these low standards may be met only in the morning, because in the afternoon high-school-age staff may be taking care of children.

Part of the reason the quality of day care in Texas is so low is that "day care has not received favorable attention from the state legislature," Vandell told the *Report*. Another reason is cutbacks in federal funding for day care, she said.

In her study of the 30 area programs, Vandell selected six for more detailed analysis—two of which were expected to be high-quality, two moderate-quality, and two low-quality.

Two sets of findings emerged that are noteworthy, said the psychology professor. Despite differences in quality, all the programs charged about the same amount. What this shows, she said, is that "parents really don't know how to evaluate day care."

Another unexpected finding was that the centers that were "moderate" in quality were more similar to those that were low in quality than to those that were high in quality.

Children in moderate- and low-quality day-care programs spent more time unoccupied and engaged more in aimless wandering than children in higher quality programs.

The quality and quantity of toys, a staff-child ratio of one teacher to six preschoolers, and a highly trained staff were other factors distinguishing good programs from bad.

---

to rest away from the group. Ask if current medical records and emergency information is maintained for each child and staff member, and if at least one staff member is trained in first aid. Are emergency numbers posted near a phone? Are fire extinguishers visible?

Check the area where food is prepared. Does it appear safe and clean? Find out what meals and snacks consist of and how they are planned.

■ Does the physical space allow for the full range of a child's needs? Each child needs personal space to keep belongings and to display projects. Separate areas are needed for quiet private play, for involvement in small groups, and for active play in large groups. You should find soft, comfortable places for children and places that encourage exploration in various program areas (art, math, science, music, drama, language, large motor development). Is the physical space aesthetically pleasing?

■ Does the learning space make sense to children? Observe whether materials are accessible to children and that children can reach them. Are materials and equipment organized so that children know where to find and return materials?

Including Parents in Evaluating Family Day Care Homes

MARY WINGET
W. GARY WINGET
J. FRANK POPPLEWELL

A 6-month study initiated in St. Paul, MN demonstrates a practical and effective method of involving parents in the formal evaluation and license renewal of family day care homes.

The responsibility for assuring minimal standards and quality care and nurturing for young children in licensed day care facilities is one shared by providers, licensing agencies, and parents. For too long, however, parents have been unintentionally excluded from the formal processes designed to assure compliance with standards. Parents, in turn, often assume that they need not be overly concerned with the issue because they believe regulations automatically provide certain guarantees.

To facilitate greater accountability on the part of licensed day care facilities, a 6-month study entitled Systematic Parent Evaluation (for Accountable Child Care) was initiated in St. Paul, MN to demonstrate a practical, effective method of parent involvement in the formal processes designed to assure regulatory compliance and quality care in licensed family day care homes [1]. The study, conducted by The Child Care Council of Ramsey County, the Ramsey County Human Services Department, and Ramsey County Family Day Care Association, was based upon the following assumptions:

1. Parents share the responsibility with providers and licensing agencies for assuring that licensed homes meet minimum standards and provide quality care and nurturing; therefore, parents should participate in the evaluation of licensed homes.
2. Parents are generally not informed about the standards that licensed family day care homes must meet; therefore, parents should be informed about these standards as part of the evaluation process.
3. Parent evaluations are useful in reinforcing strengths and correcting deficiencies in the operation of homes; therefore, the feedback from their evaluations should be shared with providers, licensing workers, trainers, and others interested in family day care.
4. Parent evaluations must be integrated into the formal system in such a way that their feedback will be used; therefore, their evaluation should be a part of the licensing renewal process.

Setting, Method, and Objectives

In 1978 there were approximately 950 family day care homes in Ramsey County (in which St. Paul is located) that provided care for about 3,000 children, i.e., 60% of all children in licensed facilities. At any given time approximately two-thirds of these homes were in use and there was an annual turnover of 20% among providers.

Reprinted with permission from *Child Welfare* 61 (4) (April 1982): 195–205.

For this study, questionnaires were sent to all parents using (or who had used within the previous 12 months) family day care homes that were applying for renewal of their licenses. Names were taken from enrollment and termination forms required by the licensing agency. Four categories of information were requested from parents: basic descriptive information, such as how long a family had used a given home; objective ratings of the provider and facility, such as safety of the outside play area; evaluation of a provider's skills relative to specific developmental age ranges, such as language development; and enumeration of strong and/or weak points of the day care home.

Information from completed questionnaires was keypunched for computer analysis on a monthly basis and average ratings were produced and summarized for each provider [2]. These "provider profiles" were then distributed to the licensing worker who analyzed them together with the written comments on the questionnaires, and then discussed them with the providers at the time of relicensing. A copy of the profile was also left with the provider. Finally, the county summary (a general overview of the parents' perceptions of licensed family day care) was distributed to county, provider, and planning groups.

The impact of parent feedback was assessed through interviews and questionnaires completed by county licensing workers and questionnaires completed by members of the Family Day Care Association's board of directors. This assessment took place 24 months after the end of the study period.

The study had three objectives: to determine parental levels of satisfaction with the care and nurturing their children received in the homes; to determine predictors of parental satisfaction with homes; and to determine the impact parental feedback had on reinforcing strengths and correcting deficiencies in the homes.

Findings

Of the 1,183 forms that were distributed 45% were completed and returned, with a variation in the monthly response rate from 25% to 60%. Because of limited staff time it was not feasible to do followup on nonresponding parents. Of those parents who did respond, 49% had used the home for more than one year and 72% were currently using the home.

Level of Satisfaction

Table 1 illustrates how parents rated providers on (1) characteristics of parenting considered to be integral to a child's social and emotional development, and (2) facility characteristics. Ratings were very positive (on a 4-point scale) in regard to providers' interaction with children and attunement to their feelings. Safe, quality facilities were also indicated.

Parents also rated specific "caring" behaviors of providers according to the age of the child for whom care was provided. Sometimes different questions were asked for each of the age groups. As can be seen from Table 2, most parents were "satisfied" or "very satisfied" (on a 5-point scale) with the care their children received.

On the other hand, parents were sometimes "dissatisfied" or even "very dissatisfied" with some aspect of care, and the average ratings of care were different for each age group. The items used to rate infant, toddler, and preschool care were not absolutely identical, but they were essentially comparable in that they sought to measure similar attributes, such as socialization and language development. Curiously, parent

Table 1

Mean Provider and Facility Ratings

Characteristics of Provider and Facility	*Mean*
Provider	
Showed sensitivity to child's feelings	3.54
Listened to and talked with child	3.61
Hit, slapped, or spanked child	1.13
Disciplined child without being threatening	3.37
Recognized child's strengths and needs	3.42
Facility	
Safe for child	3.82
Dirty and unreasonably cluttered	1.11
Safe outside play area	3.77
Supplied with books, toys, equipment	3.82

Note. n = 521. Rated on a 4-point scale: 1 = never, 2 = sometimes, 3 = usually, and 4 = always.

satisfaction seemed to decrease as the age of their children increased. Parents of infants gave an average rating of 4.62 (on a 5-point scale), as compared with 4.49 by parents of toddlers, and 4.36 by parents of preschool children. Although the infant-toddler difference and the

Table 2

Mean Caring Rating by Behavior and Age Group

Behavior	*Infant*[a]	*Toddler*[b]	*Pre school*[c]	*School- age*[d]
Held, rocked, cuddled, played with infant	4.61			
Talked, made sounds in response to babbling	4.63			
Allowed child to crawl, climb, attempt to walk	4.71			
Encouraged child to feel, taste, smell, listen, look	4.60			
Changed diapers as frequently as needed	4.59			
Participated in toilet training as parent wished		4.55		
Stimulated language development		4.48	4.38	
Provided large muscle activities		4.45	4.37	
Provided small muscle activities		4.50	4.34	
Stimulated creativity and imagination		4.34	4.33	
Supported feelings		4.46	4.26	4.28
Encouraged positive social relationships		4.66	4.46	4.48
Provided proper supervision				4.39
Arranged recreational activities				4.32
Cooperated in arranging neighborhood activities				3.99
Provided place for and assisted with homework				3.97

Table 2

Mean Caring Rating by Behavior and Age Group (continued)

n = 146 infant, 165 toddler, 240 preschool, and 151 schoolage children. Rated on a 5-point scale: 1 = very dissatisfied, 2 = dissatisfied, 3 = neither, 4 = satisfied, 5 = very satisfied.

[a] Infant = under 16 months
[b] Toddler = 16 through 30 months
[c] Preschool = 2½ through 5 years
[d] Schoolage = over 5 years

toddler-preschool difference were not statistically significant, the difference between perceived quality of infant care (4.62) and perceived quality of preschool care (4.36) was quite significant (t = 3,01, $p < .01$). Care must be taken not to let this difference detract from the fact that the average satisfaction with preschool care was still exceptionally high. To say that there is a significant difference between the two under these circumstances, then, simply means that parents using infant care are even closer to being "very satisfied" than parents using preschool care.

Other questions dealt with supplemental caring information, and communications between parent and provider. Parents indicated that providers served nutritious meals and snacks (95%), took the children on outings (76%), were dependable (99%), helped in teaching values the parent wanted learned (97%), and kept the parents informed about what the children were doing (95%). On most evenings a majority of parents (70%) talked with the provider about the child, and 3% scheduled regular conferences with the provider.

In order to directly address the question of parent satisfaction, three threshold questions were asked about enrolling/keeping the parent's child in the home and recommending the home to a friend. The responses can be seen in Table 3. (Responses to these key items were used as criterion variables in the later analysis aimed at determining the best predictors of parent satisfaction.)

Open-ended questions (What three things do you most look for when selecting a home? What were the strong points of this home? What were

Table 3

Percentage of Parents Who Would Enroll Child and Recommend Home

Would enroll/keep their child in home and would recommend home to a friend.	92%
Would enroll/keep their child in home but would not recommend home to a friend.	3%
Would not use home and would not recommend home to a friend.	5%

n = 521.

the weak points?) allowed parents to supply subjective comments that were not incorporated into the individual home summaries but were reported verbally by the licensing worker to the provider. For the county summary, the responses were coded into one of fifteen categories similar to those developed in the 1975 National Childcare Consumer Study [3]. While 484 listed strong points, only 162 parents listed a weak point. Table 4 compares the four "most important factors in selection" of a home in the national study with the "strong" and "weak" points perceived in county homes. The significance of the ranking lies in the fact that Ramsey County parents sought the same kinds of qualities as all parents in need of day care.

Predictors of Satisfaction

While the central focus of the project was to analyze the information about child care quality provided by each individual item, a secondary goal was to determine which subset of items could provide the most efficient prediction of parent satisfaction.

Table 4

Comparison of Most Important Selection Factors for Homes in National Study With Strong and Weak Points of Homes in County Study

| | | County | |
Rank National Selection Factors	Strong Points	Weak Points
1. Reliable, dependable provider	Warm, loving provider	Suitable equipment and supplies
2. Warm, loving provider	Safe, clean home	Safe, clean home
3. Safe, clean home	Personal attention for child	Educational experiences
4. Child likes type of care	Reliable, dependable provider	Personal attention for child

National selection factors are from 1975 National Childcare Consumer Study [3].

In evaluating family day care home services, the "real" predictor variables were the parenting behaviors of the provider as perceived by the parent and measured by the questions on the evaluation forms. (These behaviors were the real predictor variables because they were what actually shaped the parents' attitudes about the day care homes they used.)

The criterion measure for this analysis consisted of the responses in Table 3. In a simple and straightforward way, parents were asked if they would use and recommend a home; if they would use, but not recommend, a home; or if they would neither use nor recommend a home. This item was deemed to be a basic measure of satisfaction in that there were tangible, observable results to corroborate the responses to the item, e.g., the parent either continued to use the home or did not. (Parents who would use but not recommend the home to a friend were, for purposes of this analysis, considered to be well on the way to terminating the use of the home.)

Using the responses in Table 3 as a trichotomous criterion measure, seven stepwise multiple regressions were performed to relate seven groupings of predictor variables to the criterion. These predictor variable groupings were: provider characteristics; facility characteristics; infant caring behavior; toddler caring behavior; preschool caring behavior; school-age caring behavior; and supplemental caring and communication information.

Parents were most satisfied with a home where the provider:

1. recognized a child's strengths and weaknesses
2. had the home supplied with materials, books, toys, etc.
3. held, rocked, cuddled, and played with infants
4. supported the feelings of toddlers and preschoolers
5. provided supervision for school-agers
6. helped parents in teaching the values they wanted their children to learn

Impact of Parent Feedback

The final objective of the study was to determine the impact of parent feedback in terms of reinforcing strengths and correcting deficiencies. There was general agreement on the part of licensing workers that parent evaluation did have an impact but responses varied as to degree. The impact was shown to be highly useful in reinforcing strengths ("it raised the provider's self-worth"; "it had a snowball effect—they got better and better") but only moderately useful in correcting deficiencies ("providers were not quick in changing"). The most frequent low ratings and negative responses appeared to result from poor communication between parent and provider and/or between provider and licensing worker. The following case examples provide further insight into the use licensing workers made of the parent evaluations.

Case A. The parent indicated that the home provided no large-muscle activities, but the home actually had tumbling mats and a small gym that was used regularly. The parent feedback helped the provider realize that she needed to give parents more information about her program.

Case B. The parent stated that the provider did not regularly serve snacks and that she spanked children on occasion without the parents' permission. The licensing worker and provider discussed these matters, and a statement was signed by the provider which quoted the appropriate sections of the licensing rule and stated that she agreed to comply with it. Since the agreement was signed, there have been no indications of skipping snacks or spanking. In general, the home received and continues to receive a very satisfactory rating from parents.

Case C. The parents reported that the provider was lax in supervision and in establishing a safe place to play. The licensing worker had the same concern but no specific facts. A special visit was made by the licensing worker to discuss the problems and suggestions for improvement. As a result, the provider withdrew her request for an increase in her licensed capacity and requested help in developing a schedule of activities for the children.

Case D. The parent of an infant answered "don't know" on several questions. At the end of the evaluation the parent wrote a note saying that she realized some of these were things that she should be discussing with the provider.

Providers also viewed parent feedback in a positive light (88% indicated that they liked getting the feedback and 12% indicated that they "didn't care") but felt that it had only slight effect in reinforcing strengths and did not identify weaknesses.

When licensing workers and providers were asked whether parent evaluations should be incorporated into the state's licensing rule, 67% of the licensing workers and 50% of the providers gave a positive response.

Conclusion

Overall, parents were very satisfied with the quality of care and nurturing their children were receiving in licensed family day care homes. They found their providers to be warm and loving people who provided a safe and clean home as well as personal attention to their child. Ninety-two percent of the parents would enroll/keep their child in the home they used as well as recommend it to a friend.

There were, however, some parents who were dissatisfied with certain aspects of the home while giving it an overall high rating, and a few who were dissatisfied with the home in general. For example, 8% of the parents said they would not recommend the home to a friend. The most often cited weak point was lack of suitable equipment and supplies.

Several predictors of satisfactions were identified, including a provider's recognition of a child's strengths and weaknesses, a home supplied with toys and materials, and one that helped parents teach values they wanted their children to learn.

The parent evaluations had an impact on reinforcing providers' strengths and correcting providers' weaknesses; but while the impact was high in relation to reinforcing strengths, it was only moderate in relation to correcting weaknesses. The most frequent low ratings resulted from poor communication, both between parent and provider and between provider and licensing worker.

It was demonstrated that parent evaluation was a practical and efficient method of parent involvement in the formal relicensing process for family day care homes and that it significantly increased the assurance of regulatory compliance and quality care and nurturing in the homes.

Notes and References

1. A "licensed family care home" means a facility, usually a private dwelling unit, licensed by the state to care for up to five preschool children, including the provider's own preschool children, as well as up to 2 part-time school-age children for periods of less than 24 hours per day. Group family day care homes, which can care for up to 10 preschool children, are included in this definition for purposes of this study. A person caring for the children of only one family, for the children of relatives, for children less than 30 days per year, etc., is not required to be licensed.

2. Initial attempts to utilize packaged computer programs for summarizing data proved to be unwieldy. To better facilitate dissemination of parent feedback, a hybrid computer program (SPEACC Profile) was developed; this program was specifically oriented and suited to the purpose.

3. Rodes, Thomas W., and Moore, John C. National Childcare Consumer Study: 1975. Vol. 2. American Consumer Attitudes and Preferences on Child Care. Washington, DC: Unco, Inc., 1976.

Child Care and Disease: What Is the Link?

by Earline D. Kendall

The issue of disease spread in child care is raising questions for parents, the public, and child care and health care professionals. Is there greater chance of illness for children in child care than for children who are in other groups? What role do parents and caregivers have in providing a safe environment for children? What are some of the diseases linked to child care? Are children the only ones endangered? This article briefly reviews current research in the United States on hepatitis, some diarrheal diseases, and infections caused by H-flu, and makes recommendations for practice.

A clear trend toward increased use of infant and toddler group care is one result of changes in American family life (Bane 1976). The number of mothers who are in the work force and have children younger than age three increased from 12 percent in 1950 to 42 percent in 1978 (Zigler and Gordon 1982). The child care population has also changed: children are entering group care at younger ages than in the recent past, the number of children younger than three (and therefore in diapers) in group care has increased, and the number of children in full-time care has increased. These factors have an impact on child care and the conditions affecting children who are cared for in child care.

The problem of disease spread through these child care contacts is receiving increasing attention in medical journals (Eichenwald 1982; Pickering and Woodward 1982; Schuman 1983); the lay press (Cohn 1982a; Cohn 1982b; Goodman 1983; Howell 1983); and early childhood literature (Aronson 1983; Highberger and Boynton 1983; Silva 1980). As evidence mounted that outbreaks of bacterial, protozoan, and viral diseases are occurring in child care center environments, the language used became increasingly heated: child care centers were called culprits in disease outbreaks ("Day Care Centers Called Culprits in Disease Outbreaks in Communities" 1983); child care centers were accused of posing excessive health risks (Hadler 1983); and spread of infections contracted at child care centers was viewed as "reminiscent of the presanitation days of the 17th century" (Schuman 1983, p. 76). These concerns are based on increasing information collected and summarized through the efforts of the Centers for Disease Control (1980; 1981a; 1981b; 1982) and others (Pickering and Woodward 1982).

Child care health issues

The effects of group care on children's health have been an issue for many years. In the early part of this century, day nurseries provided group care for young children. The day nurseries reflected the health focus of nurses and social workers in such facilities. Day nurseries were seen as a means of giving children of worthy working mothers a sanitary environment. As the years went on, the emphasis on cleanliness and nutrition at the day nurseries had to accommodate concern for children's socioemotional needs, which in turn was de-emphasized when cognitive development goals came to the forefront.

Numerous studies constructed according to rigorous scientific criteria have been done, including the work of Loda, Glezen, and Clyde (1972) of the Frank Porter Graham Child Development Center. Aronson and Pizzo (1976) referred to their work as a pioneer effort on a topic where scientific information was scarce and primitive. This study found no difference in the incidence of respiratory illness in child care center children aged one month to five

Reprinted by permission from *Young Children* Vol. 38, No. 5 (July 1983): pp. 68–77. © 1983 by the National Association for the Education of Young Children, 1834 Connecticut Ave., N.W., Washington, DC 20009.

years compared to a similar group of children receiving home care. With the assistance of a variety of health care professionals, the Frank Porter Graham project demonstrated that ill children could be cared for in the child care center without increasing the risk of serious illness if the program met several conditions: stable population; ample child/staff ratios and space; and appropriate attention to careful health practices in feeding, diapering, personal care, immunizations, and prompt treatment of illnesses.

Infant and toddler group care came under particular scrutiny (Caldwell and Smith 1970; Kagan and Whitten 1970) as the number of children younger than three in group care increased. Results indicated that infants in exemplary group care did not contract significantly different diseases nor were they sick more often than similar children in home care (Collier and Ramey 1976; Kearsley et al. 1975; Loda 1980). Doyle (1975) found that center infants had a higher incidence of "flu" but concluded nevertheless that excellent group care was a viable alternative to home care.

Aronson and Pizzo (1976) extensively reviewed health and safety issues for the study of the appropriateness of the Federal Interagency Day Care Requirements (U.S. Department of Health, Education and Welfare 1978). Their study of infectious disease pointed to a relationship between child care and diarrheal diseases, tuberculosis, and infections caused by *Haemophilus influenzae* type B (H-flu). Interestingly, in light of recent findings on the spread of hepatitis A among those in contact with children in diapers who are in group care, Aronson and Pizzo's very thorough review did not disclose indications that the spread of hepatitis and child care were linked. They do cite reports on diseases spread by the fecal-oral route in day nurseries (Gelbach et al. 1973). The Centers for Disease Control's Hepatitis A—Day Care Center study (Schatz 1980) and the work by Hadler and others with the Centers for Disease Control (Black et al. 1981; Hadler et al. 1982; Williams, Huff, and Bryan 1975) were reported after the FIDCR appropriateness study was completed.

Aronson and Pizzo (1976) also analyzed

state and local group care licensing code deficiencies. States uniformly viewed licensing requirements as minimal levels of protection for children in group care. Silva (1980) cited hepatitis spread as indicative of the need for adequate standards in federally supported child care. In their 1982 Child Watch survey of state licensing officers, Kendall and Walker (submitted for publication) found licensing standards and enforcement of licensing codes to be weakening due to deregulation and economic restrictions which curtail licensing effectiveness.

Attention to health issues in day care by health professionals has been sporadic, although their interest dates back to 1945 (*Day Care: A Partnership of Three Professions*). A Committee on Day Care was under the Maternal and Child Health Section of the American Public Health Association functioned actively from 1961 to 1969, looking into health standards and health issues (Peters 1962). The American Academy of Pediatrics issued a statement on day care in 1966 outlining the role of the pediatrician (*Pediatricians and Day Care* 1966), and in 1971 published *Standards for Day Care* which included specific health recommendations. However, these were not research based.

In 1973 the American Academy of Pediatrics issued a policy statement endorsing day care (1973), and a Report of the Committee on Infectious Diseases that included a short section on day care (American Academy of Pediatrics 1982). Studies of Head Start (North 1970); the National Day Care Study (Coelen, Glantz, and Calore 1978; Ruopp et al. 1979); and the study of family day care in the United States (Fosburg 1981) report surprisingly little empirical investigation of health issues. Day care was not even listed in the *Index Medicus* until 1974 (Pickering and Woodward 1982).

Despite the paucity of research in health aspects of child care, these issues remained a concern. Califano (1978) warned teachers that classrooms could be dangerous to their health. Gillis and Sabry (1980) found child care teachers had little knowledge of nutrition. Silver (1980) suggested child health services as a basis for policy reform. Despite these and other indications of concern for and interest in health issues, a "data vacuum surrounding the issue of day care disease" ("Data Vacuum Surrounds Issue of Day Care Diseases, Epidemiologist Says" 1983, p. 5) still existed. Medical microbiological research attention to the link between child care and disease spread is now being conducted, reported, and reviewed by many who are concerned about the implications for children, parents, teachers, and communities.

Medical evidence of child care disease spread

Hepatitis

Hepatitis is a viral disease that infects the liver and causes destruction of liver cells. Like many illnesses caused by viruses, individuals can be infected without showing symptoms. Children often show little evidence of infection while adults may be very sick, with jaundice.

In 1975 *The Journal of Infectious Diseases* carried a three-year Centers for Disease Control report: "Hepatitis A and Facilities for Preschool Children" (Williams, Huff, and Bryan 1975). This article reported on hepatitis related to child care centers in ten states; "substandard" hygiene practices were found in four instances. Williams, Huff, and Bryan concluded that "transmission may not depend on substandard facilities" (p. 494), since they estimated that the ratio of asymptomatic to symptomatic children with hepatitis is 30 to 1.

In 1976, 2 outbreaks of hepatitis were reported in New Orleans (Storch et al. 1979). Outbreaks were defined as viral hepatitis in three or more households associated with the same child care center in a three-month period. A total of 11 outbreaks associated with child care was found in New Orleans in a two-year period. Of the 168 cases of viral hepatitis in the New Orleans area, 13 percent were associated with child care center contacts. Two of the diagnosed cases were children; they were diagnosed only after both their parents developed confirmed cases of hepatitis. In 44 percent of the child care related cases of hepatitis, no illness in children in the child care centers was recalled; 56 percent reported that children had gastrointestinal illness and fever. Of the child care related cases, 8 percent were child care children. Parents were at high risk if their children were one to two years old and in child care. Children in this age range were the primary carriers to infected households.

Although the children who became ill exhibited only mild symptoms, the adults to whom they carried hepatitis were often quite ill. The estimated financial cost per household was $1,952. In spite of the assumption that child care contact was a major factor in the spread of hepatitis during the two-year outbreak, and that closing infected child care centers might terminate that outbreak, no centers were closed. It was feared that closing centers would spread hepatitis to children in other child care centers as children were moved to new centers.

In 1979, Patricia Harris, the Secretary of Health, Education and Welfare; Dr. Julius Richmond, Surgeon General of the United States; and Donald Francis of the Centers for Disease Control agreed on a national study to determine the extent of hepatitis spread in child care settings. Twenty locations throughout the United States, where the counties had good hepatitis reporting systems and 40 or more cases per year, were selected for the study. As a result, the Centers for Disease Control unofficially estimated that 20 percent of all serious hepatitis A virus (HAV) cases could be linked to child care centers. Where centers are large (more than 50 children) and children are younger than two years, the percentage of HAV may be as high as 45 percent (Richmond and Janis 1982).

A Phoenix study found 30 percent of HAV related to child care (Hadler et al. 1980). In a two-year study of 279 licensed centers in Phoenix, 85 (30 percent) had three or more families affected. In centers enrolling infants younger than one year of age, 63 percent had outbreaks; in centers with children only aged one year and older, 32 percent had outbreaks; and in centers with children only two years of age and older, 2.5 percent had outbreaks (Hadler et al. 1982). Outbreaks were significantly more frequent (a) in large centers with more than 50 children, (b) in centers open more than 15 hours each day, and (c) in centers operated for profit. The introduction of hepatitis was related to the number of hours a center was open and to the ages of children served, but spread of hepatitis was found to be related solely to the presence of children younger than two years.

Since the Phoenix centers demonstrated such a clear link between child care and the spread of HAV, and had a rate of HAV ten times the national average, the effect of Immunoglobulin on HAV in child care centers was studied as a means of controlling HAV spread (Hadler et al. 1983). After 21 months of use of Immunoglobulin in child care centers that previously had HAV confirmed in one center child or employee, or in parents in at least two families, there was a 75 percent reduction of hepatitis in the community. The Immunoglobulin was administered in 91 child care centers within an average of 17 days of onset of the HAV index case. Child care directors and staff received training in specific hygiene practices and in case reporting as a part of an early detection program.

Another area where hepatitis has been a major problem is Alaska. In 1976 and 1977, Anchorage reported 116 cases of hepatitis during a nine-month period (Benenson et al. 1980). Of the cases linked to child care, 55 percent were related to one center which was modern, well managed, but which enrolled 415 children younger than three years of age. Benenson et al. conclude

> it is possible for youngsters with relatively mild symptoms of disease such as hepatitis to go unrecognized and remain in the facility during the period of infectivity. Despite the most rigid sanitary practices, fecal-oral spread of disease in a group not yet toilet trained is continually possible. It is therefore essential that persons involved in the care of young children be made aware of this potential. (p. 480)

By 1980 the Centers for Disease Control reported that 17 states had found HAV related to child care centers. Usually child care cases were linked to children from one to two years of age who showed minimal symptoms, but communicated HAV to adults at home and in the center.

Diarrheal diseases

Acute infectious diarrhea in children is usually acquired through person-to-person transmission or ingestion of contaminated food or drink; "food or waterborne outbreaks in day care centers are unusual" (Pickering and Woodward 1982, p. 48). All age groups may be affected, but the highest attack rates occur in children younger than two years. Weissman et al. (1975) found the attack rate for children younger than two years to be 82 percent, compared with 41 to 52 percent in older children. A study of giardiasis found the lowest rate was in infants confined mainly to cribs, in contrast to the highest rate found among one-year-old children who were mobile but not yet toilet trained (Keystone, Krajden, and Warren 1978).

Most diarrheal infections last only 24 to 48 hours, but some caused by different organisms can be much more serious. The major problem with diarrhea is the loss of fluid from the body tissues, which can be much more serious in small children than in adults.

A research project designed with a control group and an experimental group to determine the effects of handwashing to prevent diarrhea in child care centers was instituted for a 35-week period (Black et al. 1981). Four child care centers, all a part of a national chain of child care centers in Atlanta, were monitored: two centers had a handwashing program; two centers did not. In 1976 diarrheal illness in the four centers was monitored. The child care staff recorded daily attendance and occurrence of diarrhea for each child younger than two-and-one-half years. Diarrhea was defined as any stool judged by the child care center staff as watery or looser than usual for that child. No attempt was made to identify diarrhea at home. During the two months of baseline data collection, handwashing and toilet supervision were sporadic. Baseline stool specimens were taken for all children in the program and for all new children entering the program. During the study, stool specimens were taken from each child with diarrhea and from one other child in the group that day. Stools were examined for certain parasites, bacteria, and viruses.

At the end of the baseline period, hand-washing procedures were then instituted in the experimental centers. Staff washed hands after arriving at the day care center, before handling food, after diapering children, and when helping a child or self toilet. Children washed hands when they entered the center, used the toilet, were diapered, or were ready to eat. Bar soap and paper towels were used. Supervisors ensured that the handwashing procedure was carried out. A total of 116 children was observed during the equivalent of 2242 child-weeks.

Results reported by Black et al. (1981) indicated that even though children at control centers had less diarrhea than those at handwashing centers during the two-month baseline period, the incidence of diarrhea in the control centers was nearly twice that at handwashing centers for the remainder of the 35-week study. New children entering the control centers had diarrhea within two to four weeks after entering the program. Children not in child care centers usually have one or two diarrheal illnesses per year. Control children in this study had four diarrheal illnesses per year.

Haemophilus influenzae type B (H-flu)

H-flu is a common infecting organism and is considered responsible for much of the middle-ear infection (otitis media) seen in young children. It is also the leading cause of meningitis in this age group. The organism can be killed by antibiotics and chemotherapeutic agents, but it also can develop resistant strains, a reason some infectious disease experts worry about H-flu infection. In contrast to hepatitis and diarrhea which are spread through the fecal-oral route, infections caused by H-flu are spread by the respiratory route and are highly contagious (Eichenwald 1982).

One case study of a center in Texas with a high level of operating proficiency and cleanliness indicated that one-third of the children in the center carried the H-flu organism and that one staff member did. When various procedures failed to prevent the spread of infections caused by H-flu among the children the center was closed permanently.

The Centers for Disease Control recommend that parents be notified in writing of any case of H-flu infection in a center. The efficacy of treatment (chemoprophylaxis) in child care center related cases is less complete than for household contacts. Unless 75 percent of the contacts receive treatment, it is unlikely to be effective (Centers for Disease Control 1982). As in the case of hepatitis spread, asymptomatic carriers other than the index patient may help spread infections caused by H-flu (Eichenwald 1982). Attempts to immunize children to prevent the disease had not yet proved to be efficacious (Granoff et al. 1980).

"No major epidemic [of meningitis in this country] has occurred in the last 34 years" (Centers for Disease Control 1981a, p. 114). During the first nine weeks of 1981, 893 cases of Meningococcal disease of unspecified cause and for all ages were reported in the United States (Centers for Disease Control 1981a), in contrast to 528 for the same period in 1980 (a 69 percent increase). Only 2 percent occurred in the mid-Atlantic states; 93 percent were reported in the western and south central states. The largest increase was in Texas, Florida, and Connecticut. Clusters appeared in elementary schools, but the high risk group appeared to be those with child care contacts.

Recommendations

Recommendations from medical sources range from the specific suggestion to ban all nontoilet trained children (Eichenwald 1982) to see a broader view of the child care disease issue. Optimal health programs include preventive health care services such as health education for children, teachers, and parents; training of child care center staff in detection and prompt referral of problems, emergency and safety procedures; and referral and follow-up by health professionals (Richmond and Janis 1982).

A collaboratively designed health care program for child care centers, using the expertise of nursing and child development specialists, is recommended by Pridham and Hurie (1980). Suggestions for handwashing facilities in all diaper-changing areas in addition to those in bathrooms and food preparation areas also come from the nursing literature (Meyer 1980).

An editorial in the *Journal of the American Medical Association* (Schuman 1983) calls for "physicians as a group [to] assist daycare operators as a group in improving health standards" (p. 76). In order to address the issue of child care diseases, Michael Osterholm, Chief of the Acute Disease Epidemiology Section at the Minnesota Department of Health, is coordinating a symposium, Infectious Disease in Day Care: Management and Prevention, to be held in June 1984 in Minneapolis (personal communication, 1983). Only a "renaissance of multidisciplinary concern for new kinds of community services" (Peters 1982, p. 652) can provide the data base of information and ensure the likelihood of implementing change where problems are identified.

This review of the literature addressing the spread of disease through child care contact indicates mounting evidence that group care, especially when not carefully monitored, presents certain risks for very young children, child care providers, families, and the community. Determining the extent of the risks and the procedures necessary to mediate the risks will require the continued attention and expertise of both early childhood and health professionals.

Recommendations for practice

Conclusions based on the literature related to disease spread in day care settings include the following. As more information on the topic is made clear through additional medical microbiological research other conclusions may be drawn for day care practice.

1. Require careful and consistent attention to handwashing procedures for children and adults (Black et al. 1981). Adults should "wash hands after any toilet/diaper related activity, being careful to use a towel to turn off the water to avoid recontaminating hand surfaces with fecal material left there when turning on the tap" (Aronson 1983, p. 13). Highberger and Boynton (1983) recommended using liquid soap be-

cause it is much more sanitary, lathering well, and using friction to remove microorganisms.

2. Post procedures for diapering and feeding in areas where these activities occur (Pickering and Woodward 1982). For example, Aronson (1983) advises cleaning "all surfaces touched during diapering. . . . with a solution of one-half cup household bleach to one gallon tap water kept in a spray bottle in the diaper-changing area, but out of the reach of children" (p. 13). She also recommends using "stepstools and toilet adapters" rather than potty chairs. Additional recommendations are offered in Aronson (1983) and Highberger and Boynton (1983).

3. Separate feeding and diapering activities so that these do not occur in the same areas (Aronson 1983).

4. Place the diaper area adjacent to a sink for immediate handwashing after each diapering (Highberger and Boynton 1983).

5. Be aware that small groups of children who are still in diapers, and small centers (fewer than 50 children) provide safer environments for very young children (Hadler et al. 1982).

6. Continue staff training related to disease spread so that new staff receive information on appropriate procedures for preventing bacterial and viral disease spread and that ongoing staff practice such procedures (Aronson 1983).

7. Separate children who are in diapers from children who are not (Pickering and Woodward 1982).

8. Provide adequate paid sick leave in order for staff to have recovery time when they are ill (Peters 1983).

9. Maintain contact with medical professionals or the infectious disease control personnel in your local public health service for continuing consultation related to health issues of children (Schuman 1983).

References

American Academy of Pediatrics. "Policy Statement on Day Care." *Pediatrics* 51 (1973): 947.

American Academy of Pediatrics. *The Report of the Committee on Infectious Diseases*, 19th ed. 1982.

Aronson, S. S. "Infection in Day Care." *Child Care Information Exchange* 30 (1983): 10–14.

Aronson, S. S., and Pizzo, P. "Health and Safety Issues in Day Care." Concept paper for the Department of Health, Education and Welfare as a portion of the *Study of the Appropriateness of the Federal Interagency Day Care Requirements.* Washington, D.C.: U.S. Government Printing Office, 1976.

Bane, M. J. *Here to Stay.* New York: Basic Books, 1976.

Benenson, M. W.; Takafuji, E. T.; Bancroft, W. H.; Lemon, S. M; Callahan, M. C.; and Leach, D. A. "A Military Community Outbreak of Hepatitis Type A Related to Transmission in a Child Care Facility." *American Journal of Epidemiology* 112 (1980): 471–481.

Black, R. E.; Dykes, A. C.; Anderson, K. E.; Wells, J. G.; Sinclair S. P.; Gary, G. W., Jr.; Hatch, M. H.; and Gangarosa, E. J. "Handwashing to Prevent Diarrhea in Day Care Centers." *American Journal of Epidemiology* 113 (1981): 445–451.

Caldwell, B. M., and Smith, L. E. "Day Care for the Very Young—Prime Opportunity for Primary Prevention." *American Journal of Public Health* 60 (1970): 690–697.

Califano, J. A. "Warning! Your Classroom May Be Dangerous to Your Health." *Teacher* 95, no. 6 (1978): 20–34.

Centers for Disease Control. "Hepatitis A Outbreak in a Day-Care Center—Texas." *Morbidity and Mortality Weekly Report* 29 (1980): 565–567.

Centers for Disease Control. "Meningococcal Disease—United States, 1981." *Morbidity and Mortality Weekly Report* 30, no. 10 (1981a): 113–115.

Centers for Disease Control. "Multiply Resistant Pneumococcus—Colorado." *Morbidity and Mortality Weekly Report* 30, no. 17 (1981b): 197–198.

Centers for Disease Control. "Prevention of Secondary Cases of *Haemophilus influenzae* Type B Disease." *Morbidity and Mortality Weekly Report* 31, no. 50 (1982): 672–674.

Coelen, C.; Glantz, F.; and Calore, D. "Day Care Centers in the U.S.—A National Profile 1976–1977." In *Final Report of National Day Care Study* 3 (1978): 214, Cambridge, Mass: Abt Associates.

Cohn, V. "Day-Care Centers Infection 'Hotbed'." *The Hartford Courant* (December 12, 1982a): A10.

Cohn, V. "Day Care Diseases: A New Children's Health Problem Emerges." *The Washington Post* (November 26, 1982b): A1, A12.

Collier, A. M., and Ramey, C. T. "The Health of Infants in Daycare." *Voice for Children* 9 (1976): 7–22.

"Data Vacuum Surrounds Issue of Day Care Diseases, Epidemiologist Says." *Report on Preschool Education* (January 25, 1983): 5–6.

Day Care: A Partnership of Three Professions. Washington, D.C.: Child Welfare League of America, 1945.

"Day Care Centers Called Culprits in Disease Outbreaks in Communities." *Report on Preschool Education* (January 11, 1983): 7.

Doyle, A. B. "Infant Development in Day Care." *Developmental Psychology* 11 (1975): 655–656.

Eichenwald, H. F. "Infections in Day Care Centers." *Pediatric Infectious Disease* 1, no. 3 (1982): s66–s71.

Fosburg, S. "Family Day Care in the U.S.: Summary of Findings," U.S. Department of Health and Human Services Pub. No. (OHDS) 80-30282. Washington, D.C.: U.S. Government Printing Office, 1981.

Gelbach, S. H.; MacCormach, J. N.; Drake, B. M.; and Thompson, W. "Spread of Disease by Fecal-Oral Route in Day Nurseries." *Health Services Report* 88 (1973): 320.

Gillis, D. E. G., and Sabry, J. H. "Daycare Teachers: Nutrition Knowledge, Opinions, and Use of Food." *Journal of Nutrition Education* 12, no. 4 (1980): 200–204.

Goodman, E. "The Story of Day Care Is What's Not Going On." *The Tennessean* (January 14, 1983): 9.

Granoff, D. M.; Gilsdorf, J.; Gessert, C. E.; and Lowe, L. "*Haemophilus influenzae* Type B in a Day Care Center. Relationships of Nasopharyngeal Antibody." *Pediatrics* 65 (1980): 65.

Hadler, S. C. "Do Day-Care Centers Pose Excessive Health Risks to Children?" *Pediatric Alert* 8, no. 2 (1983): 5.

Hadler, S. C.; Erben, J. J.; Francis, D. P.; Webster, H. M.; and Maynard, J. E. "Risk Factors for Hepatitis A in Day-Care Centers." *The Journal of Infectious Diseases* 145, no. 2, (1982): 255–261.

Hadler, S. C.; Erben, J. J.; Matthews, D.; Stanko, K.; Francis, D. P.; and Maynard, J. E. "Effect of Immunoglobulin on Hepatitis A in Day-Care Centers." *Journal of the American Medical Association* 249, no. 1 (1983): 48–53.

Hadler, S. C.; Webster, H. M.; Erben, J. J.; Swanson, J. E.; and Maynard, J. E. "Hepatitis A in Day-Care Centers: A Community-Wide Assessment." *New England Journal of Medicine* 302 (1980): 1222–1227.

Highberger, R., and Boynton, M. "Preventing Illness in Infant/Toddler Day Care." *Young Children* 38, no. 2 (January 1983): 3–8.

Howell, M. "The Healthy Child: How Clean Is Clean Enough?" *Working Mother*, (January 1983): 17–19.

Kagan, V., and Whitten, P. "Day Care Can Be Dangerous." *Psychology Today* 4, no. 7 (1970): 36–39.

Kearsley, R. B.; Zelazo, P. R.; Kagan, J.; and Hartmann, R. "Separation Protest in Day-Care and Home-Reared Infants." *Pediatrics* 52 (1975): 171–175.

Kendall, E. D., and Walker, L. "Day Care Licensing: Eroding Regulations." Submitted to *Child Care Quarterly* for publication.

Keystone, J. S.; Krajden, S.; and Warren, M. R. "Person-to-Person Transmission of *Giardia lamblia* in Day-Care Nurseries." *Canadian Medical Association Journal* 119 (1978): 247.

Loda, F. A. "Daycare." *Pediatric Review* 1 (1980): 277.

Loda, F. A.; Glezen, P.; and Clyde, W. A. "Respiratory Disease in Group Day Care." *Pediatrics* 49 (1972): 428–437.

Meyer, E. H. "Nursing in a Parent Cooperative Child Care Center." *Pediatric Nursing* 5 (1980): 21–25.

North, A. F. "Project Head Start: Its Implications for School Health." *American Journal of Public Health* 60 (1970): 698–703.

Osterholm, M. Personal communication, 1983.

Pediatricians and Day Care. Evanston, Ill.: American Academy of Pediatrics, November 1966.

Peters, A. D. "Children, Communications, Communities: Enhancing the Environments for Learning." *American Journal of Orthopsychiatry* 52, no. 4 (1982): 646–654.

Peters, A. D. "The Committee on Day Care of the American Public Health Association." *The Journal of Nursery Education* 18, no. 1 (1962): 47–48.

Peters, A. D. Personal communication, 1983.

Pickering, L. K., and Woodward, W. E. "Diarrhea in Day Care Centers." *Pediatric Infectious Disease* 1, no. 1 (1982): 47–52.

Pridham, K. F., and Hurie, H. R. "A Day Care Health Program: Linking Health Services and Primary Care Nursing Education." *International Journal of Nursing Studies* 17 (1980): 55–62.

Richmond, J. B., and Janis, J. M. "Health Care Services for Children in Day Care Programs." In *Day Care: Scientific and Social Policy Issues,* ed. E. F. Zigler and E. W. Gordon. Boston: Auburn House, 1982.

Ruopp, R.; Travers, J.; Glantz, F.; and Coelen, C. *Children at the Center: Summary Findings and Implications.* In *Final Report of the National Day Care Study* 1 (1979): 251–274, Cambridge, Mass: Abt Associates.

Schatz, G. C. "Hepatitis A—Day Care Center Study Protocol." Personal communication with Day Care Program Specialist Carolyn Deal, Tennessee Department of Human Services, 1980.

Schuman, S. H. "Day-Care Associated Infection: More Than Meets the Eye." *Journal of the American Medical Association* 249, no. 1 (1983): 76.

Silva, R. J. "Hepatitis and the Need for Adequate Standards in Federally Supported Day Care." *Child Welfare* 59, no. 7 (1980): 387–400.

Silver, G. A. "Child Health Services—A Basis for Structural Reform." In *Care and Education of Young Children in America: Policy, Politics, and Social Science,* ed. R. Haskins and J. J. Gallagher. Norwood, N.J.: Ablex, 1980.

Standards for Day Care. Evanston, Ill.: American Academy of Pediatrics, 1971.

Storch, G.; McFarland, L. M.; Kelso, K.; Heilman, C. J.; and Caraway, C. T. "Viral Hepatitis Associated with Day-Care Centers." *Journal of the American Medical Association* 242 (1979): 1514–1518.

U.S. Department of Health, Education and Welfare. *The Appropriateness of the Federal Interagency Day Care Requirements: Report of Findings and Recommendations.* Washington, D.C.: U.S. Government Printing Office, 1978.

Weissman, J. B.; Gangarosa, E. J.; Schmerler, A.; Marier, R. L.; and Lewis, J. N. "Shigellosis in Day Care Centers." *Lancet* 1 (1975):88.

Williams, S. V.; Huff, J. C.; and Bryan, J. A. "Hepatitis A and Facilities for Preschool Children." *Journal of Infectious Diseases* 131 (1975): 491–495.

Zigler, E. F., and Gordon, E. W., eds. *Day Care: Scientific and Social Policy Issues.* Boston: Auburn House, 1982.

Injuries in Child Care

Susan S. Aronson, M.D.

Pediatricians, child care staff, and parents are becoming more involved in the prevention and management of health problems in child care. Child injuries are clearly one of the most significant problem areas for both group and home child care. Although there has been no thorough study of preventive strategies, my study, reported at the American Academy of Pediatrics meeting in April 1983, demonstrates that this topic demands our immediate attention because of the opportunities for preventing injury to children.

I obtained all the claims data for 1981–82 from the Forrest T. Jones Co., Inc., which manages the child care insurance policies through NAEYC's Child Care Center Student Accident Plan. The data are an incomplete view of injury in child care as many centers did not file any claims and others did not provide complete information about the kinds of injuries which occurred. The claims data, however, do indicate areas where preventive action might be taken to avoid the most serious injuries.

From 1981 to 1982, 422 claims were filed. Two-thirds of the injuries occurred on the playground. To assess the data by severity of injury, I used a geometrically progressive scale to rate the injuries.

Rating	Severity
10	Outpatient visits, exam only
12	Outpatient visits, treatment required
31	Emergency room visits, disability of less than two months
81	Emergency room visits, disability of more than two months
340	Permanent disabilities

By tabulating the severity ratings by the type of product associated with the injury, a total hazard rating was determined based on the *number* and *severity* of injuries. From the tabulation, the 11 products associated with the most frequent or more severe injuries were listed.

Product	Number of injuries	Sum of injury/ severity rating
Climbers	48	2,343
Slides	22	944
Hand toys, blocks	28	880
Other playground equipment*	11	700
Doors	14	690
Indoor floor surfaces	12	660
Motor vehicle	16	546
Swings	12	434
Pebbles or rocks	19	432
Pencils	4	403

* (Excluding swings, sandboxes, seesaws, and gliders which were listed separately)

According to this rating system, climbers were more than twice as hazardous as the next most hazardous product--slides. There are many correctable hazards represented in the top ten most hazardous products. These data have several important implications for planning early childhood environments, and for the training of staff.

1. Unsafe climbers, slides, and other playground equipment should be modified or eliminated. The U.S. Consumer Product Safety Commission suggests these modifications to make safer playgrounds: place climbing structures closer to the ground, mount them over loose fill material such as pea gravel, pine bark, or shredded tires; space all equipment far enough away from other structures and child traffic patterns to prevent collisions; cover sharp edges and exposed bolts; limit the number of children using equipment at one time; and teach children to play safely.

2. Hazardous activities require closer adult supervision than activities with a lower injury rating.

3. Architectural features such as doors and indoor floor surfaces require special attention. Doors should have mechanisms which prevent slamming or rapid closure. Full-length view vision panels will help as-

sure that small children are seen before the door is opened. Changes in floor surfaces and edges which might cause tripping should be modified. Long open spaces should be interrupted to discourage running in areas where running is dangerous.

4. Children must always travel in seat restraints in cars or vans and must follow school bus safety rules in larger vehicles.

5. Training and resources to change hazardous conditions should be made available to all staff. Injury reports should be routinely examined by trained personnel to identify and correct trouble spots. A systematic study of injury in child care centers and in home child care is needed to assist adults in making provision for the safe care of children.

Because child care services are so varied, it is difficult to generalize methods for establishing preventive measures in centers. With the increased involvement of pediatricians helping to keep parents and caregivers informed, there can be greater opportunities for the prevention of injury among children.

*   *   *

For more information and free brochures about child safety from the U.S. Consumer Product Safety Commission, call 800-638-2772.

The American Academy of Pediatrics has initiated a program/information package which will assist pediatricians in counseling parents on safety. For more information about the program contact a local pediatrician or TIPP (The Injury Prevention Program), AAP, Division of Child and Adolescent Health, P.O. Box 1034, Evanston, IL 60204, or call 800-323-0797.

The Sexual Abuse Issue: How Can Child Care Providers Respond?

A recent **Seattle Times** banner headline decried, "THE DAY CARE NIGHTMARE—Parents' worst fear about abuse is true: It can happen here." The article goes on to cite numerous examples of sex abuse in "day cares" to dramatically make its point that your child can be sexually abused in a child care setting. Only near the end of the article, buried in the back pages, did the reporter point out that the percentage of children abused in child care is in fact "minuscule"

Since the disclosure of the allegations of sexual abuse in child care centers in California, Illinois, and Texas, this issue has generated considerable attention in newspapers, magazines, television, and radio. Much of the coverage has been objective, observing that sexual abuse does occur in child care settings, but that the vast majority of abuse occurs in the home. All too often, however, coverage has been sensational and distorted, leaving the impression that sexual abuse runs rampant in child care centers. The net effect of all the attention has been to cause considerable anxiety among parents and providers alike.

To discover what child care professionals can do to allay parents' and providers' anxieties, to prevent the occurrence of abuse, and to overcome negative media attention, **Exchange** interviewed a number of child care professionals with various areas of expertise. The following are their recommendations:

The Impact on Parents and Providers

June Solnit Sale (Director, UCLA Child Care Services, Los Angeles, California): With the recent Manhattan Beach case and others in Texas and Illinois, a shadow of doubt has been cast on child care. The hysteria that has been whipped up by the media has done a great deal to make parents painfully aware of how vulnerable they are in making a child care arrangement. This same powerlessness felt by many parents has been transmitted to providers of child care. No one would agree that clear-cut acts of child abuse and neglect and sexual molestation should go unattended. But the pressure to report and the ease of doing so has raised a legitimate fear among child care providers. As a result we are in danger of losing many nurturing and loving people so desperately needed by the field.

When the Manhattan Beach case was reported, I received a phone call from a concerned man who, with his wife, owns and operates a small proprietary child care center located near UCLA. They eke out a meager living and provide loving care for 35 young children whose parents depend upon this stable, predictable environment. He wanted to know if he should sell his center, since it seemed obvious to him that it would only be a matter of time before he would be reported for sexually abusing the children in his care.

Since he was an active provider of care, there were many times when he changed children's clothes, toileted them, held and comforted them when they were hurt or ill, and rubbed their backs at nap time. If a parent or an aide or a gossipy neighbor reported him for sexual abuse, there would be little he could do to counter the report, and he would forever be suspect, whether he was cleared of the charge or not.

I have found this owner's feelings being voiced by other men and women in all parts of the state. At my own center, the male teachers had a meeting and requested that whenever a man needed to change, toilet, help with nap time, or have any intimate contact with a child, another person should be present in order to protect the teacher from possible accusations of sexual molestation. The threat to male providers seems to be greater than to females, and presents serious problems to those of us who are trying to recruit more men into the field.

Marcy Whitebook (Coordinator, Child Care Employee Project, Berkeley, California): Recent attention on sex abuse in child care centers is creating a certain self-consciousness among child care workers that is potentially detrimental. People are reexamining their feelings about being alone with

children, about hugging children, about doing intimate things with children. It also can create more tension in the already complicated relationship between parents and teachers.

There are some basic tensions between parents and teachers that are inherent in the child care setting. If you are a parent, you want flexible hours; if you are a worker, you want your day to end at a certain time. If you are a parent, you want your teacher to think your child is the most special child in the world; if you are a teacher, you have to see the specialness in all children. If you are a parent, you want your fee low; if you are a teacher, you want to be paid well.

In addition, there are psychological tensions. Most parents who leave their children in child care are ambivalent about that, and their guilt may be projected onto the provider. They may feel jealous of the affection that their children display toward their caregiver. On the other hand, teachers have ambivalence about the values and actions of particular parents, and their own personal feelings about becoming attached to the children they care for.

This psychological relationship is further strained by the issue of child abuse. As mandated reporters, child care workers always have to be looking at the child with an eye to potential abuse. Now this attention on sexual abuse has made parents suspicious of those who are taking care of their children. So in what is a complex parent-provider relationship to start with, a substantial amount of suspicion and fear is added.

Dealing with the Media

Carole Rogin (Executive Director, National Association for Child Care Management, Washington, DC): It would be a mistake for the child care community to go out and try to counteract directly any bad publicity centers have received on this issue. What centers can do is to strive to communicate an image that reflects the level of quality they are committed to and the level of service that they provide to families, and then maintain that quality and service in each and every aspect of their centers' operation.

Lana Hostetler (Chair, State Day Care Advisory Committee for the Illinois Department of Children and Family Services): The first thing we can do to combat negative press coverage is to look at techniques of prevention that will preclude, as much as possible, this sort of incident in the future. We need to work toward providing quality care for all children: by making sure as administrators that we are highly cognizant of what is needed to provide quality care—qualified staff, adequate numbers of staff, coverage by qualified staff at all times, and adequate working conditions for staff. As we hire, as we supervise, as we administer and plan programs, we must be cognizant of meeting standards or exceeding standards.

Bettye Caldwell (President, National Association for the Education of Young Children, Washington, DC): As parents and citizens we have to be concerned if even one case of sexual abuse occurs in child care. As professionals we have to be even more concerned. But we also have to help calm the hysteria that all too quickly results from such a situation, reminding people that a few isolated incidents of malfeasance do not warrant a condemnation of the entire field.

Malpractice takes place in every field: physicians and attorneys are discharged for incompetence; pharmacists are fined for cheating on Medicaid. But we do not hear a public outcry for a cessation of the use of services of other representatives of those professions because of the inadequacies of a few. This is one of the messages that we have to try to get across at these times of reversal.

Regulatory Remedies

Lana Hostetler: Legislators tend to look for quick and easy solutions to difficult problems. With the child molestation issue in Illinois, and I'm sure its true in other states as well, the legislators' first reaction was to push for a bill requiring fingerprinting and criminal identification checks on all day care center employees . Many lawmakers felt with these procedures we could breath a sigh of relief. The problem is that neither in the Chicago incident or the Manhattan Beach incident did the participants have previous convictions, so criminal checks would not have helped. We need to be sure that lawmakers and the public are not lulled into a false sense of security by such solutions. We need to convince lawmakers that such action is only one very small piece of prevention.

The criminal identification check is also very costly. It can cost as much as $15 to $20 per person. For the state of Illinois alone, just to check day care workers, it looks like a $1.2 million price tag. I think that money might be better spent in adapting the available materials on sexual abuse for use with staff and parents and children.

Gwen Morgan (Professor, Wheelock College, Boston, Massachusetts): Many people look to licensing as the way to prevent sexual abuse in centers. However, it is not a problem that can be well controlled through licensing. Licensing can help to maintain some basic level of required standards. If somebody is going to harm children to the extent that they are going to deviate from social norms significantly, there is no way you are going to be able to protect against that sort of thing through licensing requirements. It's a criminal issue—separate and apart from licensing.

However, there are two small licensing reforms that could be made that would have an impact here. First, licensing requirements could say that parents must be permitted to observe at any time that they choose. This is something that states could quite easily do, and it would make a big difference. Many licensing requirements don't say that parents are permitted to observe at all, and a surprising number say that they are permitted to observe at "mutually convenient times." California requirements, for example, simply state that "all programs must maintain close contact with parents so that the parents are informed." They never say that parents can visit or observe. Quite a few states already have such requirements. For example, Georgia requirements state, "Parents must be permitted access to all parts of the center any time that the child is in attendance."

Increasing the frequency of visits by licensing personnel would not make any difference in my opinion. Even if you decided to visit centers every week, you could still have incidents like Manhattan Beach during the time when you are not visiting. Even if you decided to visit them every day, you could still not stop it. But unannounced visits from parents would make a difference.

One other point we need to add to licensing requirements is providing parents access to other parents. If your child is expressing some fears or anxiety or unwillingness to go to a day care program, there are ten million reasons why that could be so. But if other children are expressing the same thing, then that's something parents should be concerned about. The only way parents can find that out is to talk to other parents. So if the day care programs were required to facilitate communication among parents that would be a helpful, regulatable thing that could be done through licensing.

Supervisory Responsibility

Kathleen Murray (Consultant, Child Care Law Center, San Francisco, California): Center directors bear considerable responsibility for the prevention of sexual abuse. If a director is lax in screening and hiring staff, in maintaining appropriate staffing patterns, or in supervising staff, he or she could be found liable if incidents of abuse occurred at the center. In addition, the director must adhere to provisions of child abuse reporting laws.

We now know some of the warning signs that indicate that abuse may be taking place (see **Resources**). A director should be aware of these signs, and should exercise vigilance in watching for them. Early training of staff, parents, and board members; accompanied by clear personnel procedures, would provide a supportive framework for director action should an incident occur.

June Sale: If a director is alert, sexual abuse cannot take place in the center without his or her knowledge. I don't believe that a director can not know.

In my opinion there are some directors who are afraid or unable to discuss openly the concerns that a McMartin case raises with staff and parents. They are either so concerned that their centers' reputation be clean that they are

bending over backwards to keep everything quiet, or they are uncomfortable with confronting the issue. It is important to clear the air so that parents can trust and staff can feel trusted.

If a director finds that she can't discuss this issue, she should bring someone in from the outside who feels comfortable handling these discussions in a positive way. The outreach worker from our staff, for example, has gone out to other centers to conduct discussions for directors who are not comfortable enough to do it.

Staff, Parent, Child Education

Lana Hostetler: I think it is vital that we work with staff and with parents to give them the skills to recognize telltale signs of sexual molestation. Directors, teachers and parents need to know what to look for and how to talk to children about the experiences that they are having.

We also need to work with children to help them learn that it is okay to say no to adults, that there are certain behaviors that are not acceptable whether they come from an adult within the family or an adult at the center who you trust as your teacher.

In mounting such educational efforts, I think it would be very helpful for day care people to work closely with coalitions on sexual assault, resource centers on sexual abuse, or rape information counseling centers which already exist in their community or state. Many of these organizations have developed programs and materials for adults and children on sexual molestation. Rather than trying to develop our own programs and materials, we should invite these organizations in for parent meetings, for staff training, and for sessions with children.

Informing Parents

Kathleen Murray: Many parents feel helpless and don't know where to turn when something suspicious comes up. Their discomfort and confusion may lead them to ignore the problem or to remove their child without divulging the reason. It would be useful to give parents information about where to register their concerns to help prevent harm to children remaining in the program.

It might be helpful for regulatory agencies to provide an 800 number that parents could call and be assured that follow-up would occur. The danger is that the regulatory system may not be able to cope with large numbers of parent complaints. It may be overwhelmed because agencies typically are understaffed and investigators are not trained to deal with sex abuse issues. There is also the danger of an over reaction—parents and licensing people may become so anxious that they may go on something akin to a witch hunt and damage programs in a way that would be unfortunate.

Ideally, however, licensing and child protection agencies would respond promptly, sensitively, and effectively to parental complaints, while simultaneously respecting the rights of centers. Some steps toward that ideal include improved communication among licensing, child protective services, and centers; reform of laws which impede cooperation among responsible agencies; and better training of investigators concerning the specifics of sexual abuse, the realities of child care, and the techniques for gathering credible evidence.

Lana Hostetler: In Illinois we are preparing pamphlets which spell out all the day care requirements in easy to understand lay language to be distributed to parents. Included with that will be some materials on child sexual molestation. These materials will reiterate the mandated reporting requirements and the kinds of things that parents might look for in a quality program. We are going to require that all centers distribute these materials to parents.

Reassuring Parents

Carole Rogin: One response that has repeatedly surfaced from members of our association is the need for parent involvement in the center. It is not always easy for working parents with their hectic schedules to be involved. So our centers are actively encouraging parents to come into the centers, to visit, to observe in the child's classroom, and to do it on their own schedule.

It is important to create times that are focused on the parents, on their needs and desires for information about the daily program, about the curriculum, about their child's performance in the center. But more importantly our centers are encouraging parent presence in the center at any time. Your tradeoff there, of course, is that it can be somewhat disruptive in a classroom when an activity is going on and somebody's mother walks in. But at this point in time, the advantages of that kind of openness outweigh any minor disruptions to programs that are going on.

Marcy Whitebook: If parents in your center are anxious, you should deal with these feelings in the same way you would deal with childrens' fears— by bringing them out in the open and talking about them. The center can call a parent meeting to discuss parent concerns about abuse and how to identify it, the center's philosophy about meeting children's emotional and physical needs, and the differences between nurturing and inappropriate touching.

Let parents know they are welcome to visit the center whenever they want, and to talk to you about their concerns at any time. For those parents who do not come to such meetings, you can raise these issues at parent conferences. But the most important thing is not to try to sweep these fears under the rug.

With an emotional issue like this one, I think it is especially important that staff members learn to tune into what they and the parents are feeling about one another. They must learn to act promptly and appropriately. Parents' concerns need to be dealt with before they get blown out of proportion.

Staff need training and support to enable them to recognize parental concerns, to give feedback, and to talk to parents about their children. They also must learn how to diffuse some of the tensions that develop between adults in a child care environment. Staff meetings are an excellent forum for identifying parents with whom they are having problems, and for discussing why the problems exist and what can be done to address them.

Resources

Bonnie Neugebauer (Managing Editor, **Beginnings**): There is a great quantity of resource information available and in process on the topic of sexual abuse of children. Several choices are even available targeted specifically for a preschool audience. Of course, it is always important to choose carefully, but this topic is so extremely sensitive that it is absolutely critical to select materials comfortable for all—director, staff, parents, children. Before making a choice, preview several. From the many resources I have studied, I am most comfortable with the following:

"He Told Me Not to Tell," 1979. King County Rape Relief volunteers and staff.

King County Rape Relief
305 South 43rd
Renton, WA 98055
(206) 226-0210
1-9 copies $2.50 each (includes postage and handling)
Call for bulk prices

An excellent resource for parents and teachers. Brief, informative, straightforward advice for preventing assault as well as for responding to an assault.

Adams, Caren and Fay, Jennifer. **No More Secrets: Protecting Your Child from Sexual Assault**, 1981.

Impact Publishers
PO Box 1094
San Luis Obispo, CA 93406

A more extensive resource for parents and teachers based on the work in "He Told Me Not to Tell." It includes background information and suggestions for what to say and do to prevent a crisis as well as how to handle a crisis.

Freeman, Lory. **It's My Body—A Book to Teach Young Children How to Resist Uncomfortable Touch** (illustrated by Carol Deach), 1982.

Parenting Press, Inc.
7750 31st Avenue NE Suite 411
Seattle, WA 98115
$3.00 + shipping
> (1-10 copies—$1.25)
> (11-25 copies—$2.25)
> Bulk discounts available

A simple book suitable for very young children which reinforces the idea that you don't have to let others touch you in ways you don't like.

Hart-Rossi, Janie, **Protect Your Child from Sexual Abuse: A Parent's Guide**, 1984.

Parenting Press, Inc.
7750 31st Avenue NE Suite 411
Seattle, WA 98115

$5.00 + shipping
> (1-10 copies—$1.25)
> (11-25 copies—$2.25)
> Bulk discounts available

A companion to **It's My Body** for parents (also useful for teachers). Besides positive suggestions and straightforward information, it offers activities to teach children strategies for saying "No," developing a positive self (including body) image, talking about feelings, and learning decisionmaking. Many activities could be used in a child care program as well as in a home.

Dayee, Frances S. **Private Zone: A Book Teaching Children Sexual Assault Prevention Tools** (illustrated by Marina Megale), 1982.

The Chas. Franklin Press
18409 90th Avenue W
Edmonds, WA 98020

A straightforward, non-threatening book for children based on the idea that your genital area is yours alone and is not to be touched by others (except doctors and parents, with your permission). Note: This is a different approach from **It's My Body**. You must determine what is appropriate for your situation.

You may also want to look at **Safety Zone: A Book Teaching Child Abduction Prevention Skills** by Linda D. Meyer, 1984, by the same publishers.

Talking About Touching with Preschoolers, 1983 (adapted by Margaret Schonfield from **Talking About Touching: A Personal Safety Curriculum** by Ruth Harms and Donna James).

Committee for Children
PO Box 51049
Seattle, WA 98115
$35.00 + $3.00 postage and handling
(Washington residents add 7.9% sales tax)
(206) 524-6020

A personal safety curriculum adapted just for preschoolers. It includes lessons, illustrations, and teacher's guide. Topics include the child's right to his or her own body, assertiveness skills, and who and how to tell. The full curriculum takes 3 to 6 weeks, and becomes explicit describing specific situations. It would be possible, for those who choose to give less explicit information, to use a portion of the lessons and adapt the curriculum to need.

A Time for Caring: The School's Response to the Sexually Abused Child.

Color film, 28 minutes
A Profile Film, Lawren Productions
Mendocino, CA

Although written for public school staff, the information could provide an excellent training tool for child care staff.

Linn, Susan. **Some Secrets Should Be Told,** 1982.

Color film, 12 minutes
Family Information Systems and Resource Communications, Inc.

A very sensitive conversation among two puppets, a duck and a lion, and ventriloquist Susan Linn about sexual abuse. Presentation is direct and supportive, and encourages children to tell a trusted adult. Suitable for young children.

Bailey, Patti. **Sexual Abuse Prevention Curricula: Where to Begin.**

An extensive bibliography of resources available on sexual abuse. Revised version available by October 12, 1984 ($2.00).

Patti Bailey, Incest Treatment
Washington County Children's Services Division
1665 SE Enterprise Circle
Hillsboro, OR 97123
(503) 648-8951

Resource Centers. These ten federally funded regional resource centers provide information, consulting, and training services on child abuse. They are also a source for bibliographies, books, films, and other resources for preview or loan (free or small service fee).

● New England Resource Center for Children and Families, Boston, Massachusetts, (617) 232-8390

● Region II Resource Center for Children and Youth, Family Life Development Center, Ithaca, New York, (607) 256-7794

● Region III Resource Center for Children, Youth, and Families, Richmond, Virginia, (804) 257-6231

● Southeastern Resource Center for Children and Youth Services, Knoxville, Tennessee, (615) 974-6015

● Region V Resource Center on Children and Youth Services, Milwaukee, Wisconsin, (414) 963-4184

● Region VI Resource Center on Children, Youth, and Families, Austin, Texas, (512) 471-4067

● Region VII Consolidated Regional Resource Center, Iowa City, Iowa, (319) 353-4791

● Region VIII Family Resource Center, Denver, Colorado, (303) 753-2886

● Region IX Resource Center for Children and Youth Services, Los Angeles, California, (213) 224-3283

● Northwest Resource Center for Children, Youth, and Families, Seattle, Washington, (206) 543-1517

Hotline service. The National Child Abuse Hotline-Referral Service provides a number available to both parents and providers with concerns about sexual abuse of a child. This service provides crisis intervention and referral to appropriate local agencies.

Call: (800) 422-4453

Selected Bibliography

There is a wealth of book-length material on the subject of day care. Books are being written by professionals as well as by laypersons on almost all aspects of this diverse topic from college instruction of day care professionals to planning and preparing meals for dozens of preschoolers in center-based day care settings. The selections listed in this bibliography have been included due to their recentness of publication and because of their potential usefulness to the audience for whom this book has been written. The entries are divided into 2 sections (books, and documents and reports), are alphabetized by author (or title if there is no author), and are annotated to provide additional information.

BOOKS

Alston, Frances K. *Caring for Other People's Children.* Baltimore, MD: University Park Press, 1984.
This is a comprehensive and practically oriented book for the individual providing family day care. The business aspect of day care is discussed using examples of forms for record keeping. The majority of the book offers a wide range of activities for children of various developmental levels. Additional chapters speak to special needs of day care providers such as providing discipline, caring for a sick child, carrying out emergency procedures, monitoring nutrition, and providing for the special or exceptional child.

Baden, Ruth K., et al. *School-Age Child Care: An Action Manual.* Boston: Auburn House, 1982.
This comprehensive text addresses the problems of after-school day care. Much of the initial information is based on a survey of existing programs. One section of the book addresses the multitude of problem areas involved in establishing and implementing a program such as establishment of policies, legal issues, personnel, budget, and publicity. Another segment of the book concerns the day-to-day operation of such a program. An annotated bibliography is included as well as additional information in the appendix.

Blum, Marian. *The Day-Care Dilemma: Women and Children First.* Lexington, MA: Lexington Books, 1983.
All-day day care programs and the middle-class professional parents who typically use them are the focus of this book. It presents women and children as victims of the economic realities of providing child care. Possible solutions are proposed.

Center for Systems and Program Development, Inc. *A Parents' Guide to Day Care.* Washington, DC: U.S. Department of Health, Education, and Welfare, 1980.
This guide was published by the U.S. Department of Health, Education, and Welfare to assist parents in making child care decisions. Included: what constitutes quality day care, procedures for making day care arrangements, possible solutions to problems commonly encountered, and resources. This is a clearly written pamphlet offering parents practical information on day care and providing criteria in checklist format to assist in evaluating possible day care options.

Copeland, Tom. *Basic Guide to Record Keeping and Taxes.* 6th ed. St. Paul, MN: Toys n Things Press, 1984.
This is an update of earlier editions that provides current information on record keeping and taxes for family day care providers. Specific guidelines are included for recording various expenses. Illustrations are provided using sample forms. Necessary tax forms are explained and directions given for completing them.

Deacon, G. *Kid Tested Menus with Kitchen and Luncheon Techniques for Day Care Centers.* North Wilkesboro, NC: Gold Crest, 1981.
This practical little book covers lunchroom operation and menu planning and buying. The majority of the text is comprised of menus that will serve approximately 40 preschoolers. Each recipe is on a separate page and lists ingredients and procedures. Recipes are grouped into the following categories: main courses and go-togethers, vegetables/salads, desserts, and happy snacks.

Dreskin, William, and Dreskin, Wendy. *The Day Care Decision: What's Best for You and Your Child.* New York: M. Evans, 1983.
As former directors of a day care center, the authors draw on their experiences and on recent research to aid parents in making day care choices. The first portion of the book discusses childrens' development and day care, the second looks at day care from the parent's perspective, and the third compares the family here and abroad.

Eliason, Claudia, and Jenkins, Loa T. *A Practical Guide to Early Childhood Curriculum.* 2d ed. St. Louis, MO: C.V. Mosby, 1981.
Curricula appropriate for preschoolers is the focus of this book. The text is separated into such various curricular areas as science, language, prereading, premath, art, and music. A wealth of activities are provided as well as suggestions for making and using materials.

Endsley, Richard C., and Bradbard, Marilyn R. *Quality Day Care: A Handbook of Choices for Parents and Caregivers.* Englewood Cliffs, NJ: Prentice-Hall, 1981.
This guide is designed to aid parents in selecting day care programs for their children. It includes an overview of day care today and suggestions for evaluating various day care programs. Also discussed are physical space and program needs, health and safety needs, parental involvement, and selection guidelines. A chapter is also included on disabled children in day care. Selected references on day care make up the appendix.

Griffin, Elinor F. *Island of Childhood: Education in the Special World of Nursery School.* New York: Teachers College Press, Columbia University, 1982.
The needs of 3- and 4-year-olds are examined in the first portion of the book, focusing particularly on the child's relationships with the nursery school teacher and with other children. The second half of the book discusses means of providing for those needs through curricula.

Ispa, Jean. *Exploring Careers in Child Care Services.* New York: Rosen Publishing Group, 1984.
This text explores jobs and careers in day care. Each chapter specifies and describes a particular setting such as private home care, day care centers, after-school care, summer camp, and group home care. Suggestions are given for finding a job.

Lombardo, Victor S., and Lombardo, Edith F. *Developing and Administering Early Childhood Programs.* Springfield, IL: Charles C. Thomas, 1983.
This text offers a comprehensive look at programs for preschool-age children. It is written for early childhood teachers, care givers, group supervisors, administrators, and parents. Issues addressed include meeting regulatory agency requirements, developing the indoor facility, developing the playground facility, recruitment of personnel, characteristics of young children, public relations, and finances. It includes samples of forms that could be used in administering a program. There is also a listing of audiovisual materials to assist in teacher training.

Mitchell, Grace. *The Day Care Book: A Guide for Working Parents to Help Them Find the Best Possible Day Care for Their Children.* Briarcliff Manor, NY: Stein and Day, 1979.
As the title implies, this book is written for the parent who wants to have a knowledgeable basis from which to make day care decisions. The author, in compiling this book, visited over 150 child care centers in 22 states. It is written from a personal perspective and includes many experiences from individuals encountered. Topics included are choosing child care, a good environment for young children, the daily program, the caregivers, resources for child care, and the working parent.

Moore, Gary, et al. *Recommendations for Child Care Centers.* Milwaukee, WI: Center for Architecture and Urban Planning, 1979.
The purpose of the study that culminated in this guide was to develop and design criteria for several types of child care centers and outdoor play environments. Eight military and 15 civilian child care facilities across the United States and Canada were studied and 175 books and nearly 1,000 articles reviewed. Topics covered are the nature of child care programs and facilities, recommended changes in existing policy, and planning and design. This is a comprehensive planning guide that covers many aspects of child care.

Morgan, Gwen G. *Managing Day Care Dollars: A Financial Handbook.* Cambridge, MA: Steam Press, 1982.
This handbook is written as a guide for administrators who are responsible for the financial management of a day care center. It provides information on budget, cash flow, monitoring and accounting, and meeting tax obligations. A glossary of financial management terms is included as well as a section on resources, which provides names and addresses of organizations offering information on guidance in the area of finance and accounting.

Murphy, Karen. *A House Full of Kids: Running a Successful Day Care Business in Your Own Home.* Boston: Beacon, 1984.
This is a practically oriented book for individuals involved in home day care. It outlines many of the specifics surrounding licensing, fees, selection of children, care of infants, eating habits, toilet training, behavioral problems, and equipment and playthings. The appendix includes handouts for parents on sexuality, and a children's book list.

Robinson, Nancy M., et al. *A World of Children: Daycare and Preschool Institutions.* Monterey, CA: Brooks-Cole, 1979.
This book has been written primarily for professionals in the fields of early childhood education, child development, and day care administration. It addresses such basic issues concerning child care as rationale, goals, administrative issues, and organization and staffing. A significant portion of the book involves detailed descriptions of early day care in selected eastern and western European countries. The book concludes with a set of recommendations based on the various day care alternatives reviewed and the needs of the American family.

Sciarra, Dorothy J., and Dorsey, Anne G. *Developing and Administering a Child Care Center.* Boston: Houghton Mifflin, 1979.
This is a basic comprehensive text covering various aspects of day care. Some of the topics included are assessing community need; licensing and certifying; handling financial matters; developing, equipping, and staffing a center; enrolling children; and managing food, health, and safety programs. Examples of several forms used in registering children and keeping financial records are included.

Taylor, Katharine W. *Parents and Children Learn Together.* 3d ed. New York: Teachers College Press, Columbia University, 1981.
This text focuses on parent cooperative nursery schools where parents establish and staff their own school. A great deal of the book deals with the emotional, social, and creative needs of the children and how these might be met. The remainder describes means of developing and extending parent cooperative nursery schools.

Travers, Jeffrey, and Goodson, Barbara D. *Research Results of the National Day Care Study.* Cambridge, MA: Abt Books, 1981.
The National Day Care Study was commissioned in 1974 by the Office of Child Development (now titled the Administration for Children, Youth and Families). This volume is intended to provide

professionals with a description of the methods used in the study and the findings relating to characteristics of day care centers and experiences of the children served.

Tronick, Edward, and Greenfield, Patricia. *Infant Curriculum—The Bromley-Health Guide to the Care of Infants and Young Children.* Rev. ed. Santa Monica, CA: Goodyear Publishing, 1980.
Infant Curriculum is a comprehensive resource for day care providers and parents. It outlines the sequences of child development and suggests activities appropriate for each stage. Toys and other materials are described for their usefulness in teaching specific skills. Organizing and scheduling activities are addressed.

Zigler, Edward F., and Gordon, Edmund W., eds. *Day Care: Scientific and Social Policy Issues.* Boston: Auburn House, 1981.
This book is a collection of articles on day care from the perspectives of psychologists, psychiatrists, economists, pediatricians, public health workers, and politicians. The first part of the book focuses on theoretical and social science issues, the second is from the legislators' perspective, and the third deals with social policy issues. Several specific topics included are infant day care, federal day care regulations, costs, health care services, and school-age child care.

DOCUMENTS AND REPORTS

Administration of Child Care Programs: Business Management. Instructor's Guide. Austin, TX: Texas Education Agency, Department of Occupational Education and Technology, 1983. 268 p. (ED 241734 or EDRS)
This guide is designed for postsecondary instruction of child development; a student laboratory manual is available separately. Students are introduced to general competencies and business management aspects of child care program administration. Introductory materials discuss the use of materials and guidelines for evaluating students. Each unit includes performance objectives, a list of references, suggested classroom experiences, and a unit test composed of multiple-choice and essay questions. Transparency masters and handouts can be reproduced as needed. Appendices include a glossary, glossary test, answer keys, and a 9-page bibliography which includes possible textbooks.

Administration of Child Care Programs: Business·Management. Student Laboratory Manual. Austin, TX: Texas Education Agency, Department of Occupational Education and Technology, 1983. 148 p. (ED 241735 or EDRS)
This manual was designed as a laboratory experience guide and workbook to expose postsecondary students to general competencies and business management aspects of child care program administration. Units cover general competencies, regulations and legal concerns, personnel, and finances. Each unit includes performance objectives, an overview of basic concepts of the unit topic, and suggested readings for in-depth study. Lab experiences include both observation and participation assignments. Instructor

evaluation forms and a student checklist are provided. Also included are guidelines for successful lab experiences, a glossary, and a 15-item bibliography.

Alisberg, Helene R. *Public/Private Partnership—A Cost Effective Model for Child Day Care Services.* West Hartford, CT: United Way of Connecticut, 1984. 15 p. (ED 242422 or EDRS)
This article deals with the trend of corporations providing child care support through subsidies to low-income employees or through community facilities, parent education, and information and referral (I&R) services. The 1981 Economic Recovery Tax Act and Dependent Care Assistance Program are discussed as legislative acknowledgement of the public need for assistance in child day care services. The Corporate Consortium for Child Care in Hartford, Connecticut, is used as a model I&R service, and its operation and programs provided are described in detail.

The Bananas' Manual on Event Child Care. Oakland, CA: Bananas Inc., 1982. 53 p. (ED 238556 or EDRS)
The manual, written for individuals or groups, provides a step-by-step guide to the implementation of day care during special events such as fund raisers and workshops. Included is information on staff, site, insurance requirements, instruction on preparation of business forms, meeting the unique needs of children, discipline, scheduling, activities, equipment, food, and emergency and security precautions. Also discussed are special care for each age group, evaluations, saying goodbye to children, and final clean-up. Sample forms for maintaining records for the children and the program are included.

Calder, Judy. *Building a Special Needs Component into Your Child Care Resource and Referral Services.* Oakland, CA: Bananas Inc., 1983. 132 p. (ED 239744 or EDRS)
Designed to provide information on child care options for children with special needs, this manual discusses the criteria necessary to implement services. It is divided into 5 sections, each dealing with specific issues including questions regarding referrals, resources, and benefits for the disabled child and family; 7 action areas for program involvement; parenting the special child; relevant legislation; training curricula; and trainer resources. An extensive appendix includes an agency mail survey, a parent survey, a telephone questionnaire, a child care provider questionnaire, a special needs cataloging form, and support services file categories. Three pocket guides are also included.

Checkett, Donald. *Starting a Day Care Center: The Day Care Center Handbook.* St. Louis, MO: Child Day Care Association of St. Louis, 1982. 84 p. (ED 225648 or EDRS)
Designed to be of help to individuals and groups seeking to establish a day care center in the metropolitan St. Louis area, this manual calls attention to important and basic information which must be taken into account. Commonly used terms referring to organized preschool programs are defined, and topics covered include determining location and size of day care center; obtaining city permits and state licenses; budgeting and advertising; federal, state, and city taxes; curriculum models; guidelines for day care operation; board/executive relationships; and equipping the day care center.

Collins, Natalie Madgy, et al. *Business and Child Care Handbook.* Minneapolis, MN: Greater Minneapolis Day Care Association, 1982. 80 p. (ED 226856 or EDRS)
Intended as a resource for corporate and industrial managers, employee groups, and others, this handbook provides basic discussion of child care and offers a guide for decision making. The first chapter is a brief introductory discussion of motives for becoming involved with child care. Other chapters include discussion of the phenomenon of the working mother, changes in the composition of the work force and the need for child care, direct and indirect child care program options, costs of child care, a business and child care project needs assessment system, and the history of employer involvement in child care services in the United States. Appendices include a glossary of terms, names and addresses of sponsors providing child care options, a directory of child care services and resources, an annotated list of federal and Minnesota state legislative acts relating to child care, several fact sheets, and a brief list of compiled bibliographies.

Fowler, Dora. *A Guide to Effective Administration in Day Care.* Palatine, IL: Associates in Human Development, Inc., 1983. 275 p. (ED 242440 or EDRS)
This book contains a brief section concerning elements of the management process as well as chapters dealing with personnel, staff orientation, staff inservice training, enrollment, classroom management, curriculum, health maintenance, and center management. Numerous forms that can be used and adapted by practitioners have been included. Topics discussed range from hiring and conducting performance reviews, staff inservice training, enrollment materials and classroom management, curriculum based on early childhood principles and concepts, health maintenance materials, and insurance for centers.

Houston, Sandra T. "Child Care in the 80's: A Brief Report on Public School Involvement." Paper presented at the Annual Conference of the Southern Association of Children under Six, March 6–10, 1984, Lexington, KY. 13 p. (ED 243578 or EDRS)
Data concerning public school involvement in providing child care services in 14 southern states were obtained through questionnaires sent to state superintendents or commissioners of education in each state. In addition, questionnaires were sent to the superintendents of the 142 school districts in North Carolina. The paper focuses mainly on findings in North Carolina because information on public school child care in other southern states was too limited to have a meaningful interpretation. All

states responding were involved in providing child care services of at least one type, and most felt the need for greater involvement in half-day prekindergartens. Addresses of state departments of education surveyed as well as locations and types of child care services reported in North Carolina are included in the report.

Long, Thomas J., and Long, Lynette. *Latchkey Children.* Urbana, IL: Clearinghouse on Elementary and Early Childhood Education, 1983. 40 p. (ED 226836 or EDRS)
This article is a review of current research dealing directly or indirectly with school-age latchkey children. Research implications were related to the following questions: Are latchkey children at risk? How much risk and in which areas? Are there factors that mitigate or lead to greater risk? What are the long-term effects of the latchkey experience? Intervention strategies are briefly discussed.

Rooney, Teresa. *Who Is Watching Our Children? The Latchkey Child Phenomenon.* Sacramento, CA: California State Legislature, Senate Office of Research, 1983. 48 p. (ED 243598 or EDRS)
This report explores the latchkey dilemma and reviews possible effects this situation may have on the physical and psychological well-being of children. Topics discussed include emergence of the problem and availability of child care, problems and consequences for children left alone, a description of the scope of the problem, and an executive summary. California's role in school-age child care through direct and indirect subsidies and licensing activities is discussed, and a bibliography is appended.

Stark, Giovanna. *There Is a Choice: Choosing Good Infant and Child Day Care. Final Report and Executive Summary.* Sacramento, CA: California Child Development Program Advisory Committee, 1984. 8 p. (ED243593 or EDRS)
This article describes the project to educate day care consumers about locating quality day care for infants and children that was completed by the Child Development Program Advisory Committee on a one-year grant from the Department of Health and Human Services. Project objectives focused on inservice training for health practitioners as well as providing information to parents in maternity wards and clinics. Information was disseminated through inservice training for health educators, professionals, and pediatric nurse practitioners; videocassette presentations and printed materials for new parents; and local meetings. The project established a link between parents and community child care resources.

Appendices

Appendix A:
National Survey of Family Day Care Regulations: Summary of Findings

by Diane Adams

July, 1982

A survey of all 50 states regarding the status of family day care regulations took place in February/March, 1982. The author is analyzing state policies as part of a policy analysis at the Bush Institute for Child and Family Policy, University of North Carolina, Chapel Hill, N.C. All states (100%) responded to the telephone survey, plus the Virgin Islands, Puerto Rico, and the District of Columbia. The following data are from the survey. (The rapid change occurring in state day care regulations causes some of this information to be out of date already; such changes will be noted where possible.)

1. Number of states and territories:

54 (including Guam)

2. Number of children (capacity) in regulated/licensed child care facilities:

2,795,800 (includes the capacity of full-day centers, part-day centers, Head Start, family day care homes, group family day care in all states)

3. Number of full- and part-day *centers*:

50,120

4. Number of regulated (licensed, registered, approved/certified) family day care homes:

137,865

The most frequently cited figures are that there are about 1 million places in day care centers (*Children at the Center*, 1979). This current survey shows more than twice that many places; it is unknown whether this report means a 50% increase or whether the previous study did not include part-day preschools. The 1979 figures showed 18,000 centers. Again, these figures may not have included the many part-day programs in states. The number of regulated homes seems to be in agreement with estimates (National Day Care Home Study, 1981) that no more than 10% of homes are regulated. That study estimated there are 1.3 million family day care homes in the country; 137,000 would be just over 10% who follow the regulatory law.

5. State family day care regulations (N=54)

None (except for publicly purchased care): Arizona, Louisiana, New Jersey, Ohio, West Virginia

License (starting with 1 child=18; starting with 2-3-4 children=12; starting with 5-6 children=5): Alabama, Alaska, Arkansas, California, Colorado, Connecticut, Delaware, D.C., Guam, Florida, Hawaii, Idaho, Illinois, Indiana, Kentucky, Minnesota, Mississippi, Missouri, Nevada, New Hampshire, New Mexico, New York, North Dakota, Oklahoma, Puerto Rico, Rhode Island, Tennessee, Utah, Vermont, Virginia, Virgin Islands, Washington, Wisconsin, Wyoming

Register (mandatory=8, voluntary=3; only two states start registration with 3-4 children, all the rest start with 1 child): Georgia, Iowa, Massachusetts, Michigan, Montana, Nebraska, North Carolina (no standards), Oregon, Pennsylvania, South Dakota, Texas, Maryland

Both License and Register (depending on whether caring for publicly-funded children, or an option for providers): Kansas, Maine, South Carolina

See Appendix 1 for a complete state and territory description. Note that Georgia and Maryland are two states that have changed status since February (Georgia to mandatory registration, Maryland from licensing to registration).

While 31 states and the 3 territories and D.C. have licensing, many states are considering registration and/or have registration legislation pending. If these pass, within the next year half the states might register homes.

6. The Costs of Regulating

Using an estimated figure (based on the actual regulatory budgets of 8 states averaged), taken times the number of licensing personnel, we find a total of $46,812,000 spent in 1981 to regulated all day care. Only a portion of this is used to regulate family day care. Large states (California with 198 licensing workers, Texas with 199), of course, spend considerably more than medium-sized states (such as Michigan with 72 workers and Alabama with 76). Small states (Nevada with 1 licensing supervisor and Idaho with 9 workers) have a small number of regulated facilities.

What cannot be estimated from these budget estimates is what it costs to register homes as opposed to license homes. A 1977 Michigan report cites lower costs with registration than with licensing (Registration of Family Day Homes, 1977). States that register may have initial costs that become amortized as many more homes enter the registration system, so that more licensing workers are not needed proportionately.

Below are some examples of ratios of licensing workers to regulated homes.

Register	**License**
(Ratio of workers to homes)	*(Ratio of workers to homes)*
Massachusetts 1:231.8	Alabama 1:32.8
Oregon 1:123.5	Connecticut 1:92
Texas 1:119.7	Delaware 1:96

These data do not necessarily "prove" that registration would stretch the licensing worker load. Colorado, for example, shows 23 workers for 8330 licensed homes (a ratio of 1:362), while Pennsylvania, which recently moved to registration, shows 42 workers for 1980 registered homes (a ratio of 1:47).

7. Legislation

Twenty-five states have some proposed day care legislation pending (or enacted this session). Legislation regarding ratios, charging fees for certification of centers and homes, exempting church-sponsored or "educational" preschools, and family

day care registration are among the topics proposed for legislative change.

Nine states (D.C., Kentucky, Nebraska, North Carolina, North Dakota, Rhode Island, Utah, Vermont, Wyoming) are currently undertaking a comprehensive examination of day care in the state. Georgia has just completed such a study; Wisconsin is studying all children's issues—including day care.

Specific information about day care legislation could be obtained from Legislative Reference Bureaus in Indiana, Iowa, Kentucky, Michigan, Mississippi, Missouri, New Mexico, Washington, and West Virginia—among the 25 states with proposed legislative changes.

8. Purchasing day care for subsidized families (N=51 50 states + D.C.)

Since the demise of the Federal Interagency Day Care Requirements (FIDCR), states now use their own licensing and/or registration standards (or certification standards alone) for purchasing care.

Thirty states (58%) use their licensing or registration standards as the purchasing standards for family day care; 13 states (25%) have a different certification or approval standard from basic licensing or registration; 8 states (16%) use basic licensing or registration plus some added standards for purchased care. The following table outlines the purchasing standards:

Same as licensing (L) or registration (R) standard for purchase (N=30)
Alabama (L), Alaska (L) (does not purchase Title XX), Colorado (L),
Florida (L), Georgia (R), Hawaii (L), Idaho (L), Illinois (L), Indiana (L), Iowa (R), Kansas (L & R), Kentucky (L), Maine (L & R),
Maryland (R), Massachusetts (R), Michigan (R), Minnesota (L), Missouri (L), Montana (R), Nevada (L), North Dakota (L), Oklahoma (L), Oregon (R), Pennsylvania (R), Rhode Island (L), South Carolina (L & R),
Utah (L), Vermont (L), Washington (L), Wyoming (L)

Different certification or approval standards from basic licensure or registration (N=13)
Arizona, Louisiana, New Jersey, Ohio, W. Virginia - no other standards
Connecticut (L), Mississippi (L), New Mexico (L), New York (L), North Carolina (R), Texas (R), Virginia (L), Wisconsin (L)

Basic licensing or registration, plus some added standard for purchase (N=8)
Arkansas (L), California (L), Delaware (L), D.C. (L), Nebraska (R),
New Hampshire (L), South Dakota (R), Tennessee (L)

Only 4 of the states using a registration system feel they must use a different standard or some added regulation for purchase of care.

9. Child Care Food Program (CCFP)

The CCFP requires a home to be regulated and part of an umbrella sponsoring agency in order to participate. Respondents queried about the impact of the CCFP in bringing more community family day care providers into the regulatory system said that the food program has been a strong influence in increasing the number of regulated homes:

(N=18) A great deal- Alabama, Alaska, Arizona, Connecticut, Georgia, Kansas, Kentucky, Minnesota, Mississippi, Montana, Nebraska, New Hampshire, North Dakota, Oregon, South Carolina, Washington, Wisconsin, Wyoming

(N=18) Some- Arkansas, Colorado, D.C., Florida, Idaho, Illinois, Iowa, Maine, Massachusetts, Missouri, New Mexico, North Carolina, Ohio, Pennsylvania, South Dakota, Utah, Vermont, W. Virginia

(N=12) Not very much- Delaware, Hawaii, Maryland, Michigan, Nevada, New Jersey, New York, Rhode Island, Tennessee, Texas, Virginia, Virgin Islands

(N=3) Not sure- California, Indiana, Puerto Rico

(N=2) Absolutely none- Louisiana, Oklahoma

10. The Role of Regulations

As to why the licensing officials believe family day care providers follow the regulatory law, status and prestige is foremost. A rank-ordering of the most frequently-given reasons why licensors think providers become licensed or registered is given below:

1. Status (prestige reason)
2. To receive public dollars (Title XX or Child Care Food Program, for example)
3. To obey the law (a legal reason for law-abiding citizens)
4. To receive training and technical assistance (when available)
5. Professionalism
6. Information and referral (publicity) possibilities
7. For business benefits (tax benefits)
8. In order to advertise legally
9. For contacts with other providers

11. Enforcement

Twenty-four states say they have "very much" enforcement of their regulations for family day care; 19 say they have "some"; 7 say they have "very little"; 3 believe they have none at all or there was no answer. (N=53 states and territories).

12. Do the Regulations Improve Quality of Care?

Fifteen states felt their family day care regulations improved the quality of care ("strongly agree"), 20 had mild agreement with this statement, 7 mildly disagreed, 5 strongly disagreed, 1 was unsure, and there were 3 no answers.

As to exactly how the regulations might improve quality, states had three basic categories of answers: the regulations raise awareness of what constitutes good child care (the regulations were seen as "educational"), they were seen as "better than nothing," or the regulations did not do much one way or the other. The following states are grouped according to the category of response:

(N=26) Regulations raise awareness of good care: Arkansas, Colorado, Connecticut, Delaware, Georgia, Illinois, Indiana, Iowa, Kentucky, Maine, Massachusetts, Missouri, Nebraska, Nevada, New Hampshire, New Mexico, New York, North Dakota, Oklahoma, Pennsylvania, Puerto Rico, South Carolina, Texas, Utah, Washington, West Virginia

(N=11) Regulations are better than nothing: Alabama, D.C., Hawaii, Idaho, Kansas, Michigan, Mississippi, Oregon, Rhode Island, South Dakota, Virginia

(N=11) Regulations do not do much one way or the other to improve quality: Alaska, California, Florida, Louisiana, Montana, North Carolina, Ohio , Tennessee, Virgin Islands, Wisconsin, Wyoming

(N=3) No answer: Arizona, Maryland, Vermont

(N=1) Regulations give the power to revoke/get rid of bad care: Minnesota

13. Policy options for regulating family day care homes

The most frequent response to the policy options favored licensing systems, which then would in turn regulate homes. (Only 14 states currently do this, another 10 could under state statute). This option was often given as a policy choice with some other regulation, such as licensing. The following is how licensors ranked the policy options on an overall basis:

Rating (1=low, 7=high)

1. License family day care agencies or systems	6.16
2. Have graded licensing for homes, levels of quality	4.36
3. Traditional licensing	4.17
4. No regulations at all for homes	3.85
5. Certification of homes (only where care is purchased)	3.48
6. Registration (no standards)	3.08
7. Registration (with standard)	2.96

Only 7% of the licensing officials put licensing as their first choice (65% of states license homes). Only 6% put registration as a first choice. It would appear that licensing officials are willing to explore all the policy options, and would like to see the regulatory burden shared with some agencies that could be monitored perhaps more easily than individual homes. The fact that registration is "last" overall may mean it is less well understood by many licensing officials.

In 51% of the cases, the preferred policy option matched the current policy in the state; 49% said their preferred option did not match current policy.

This summary shows several important findings about family day care regulations as they are currently operating in the United States. First, there is much transition, as states move from licensing to registration, enact new standards for purchase of care with the demise of FIDCR, or "lose" some of their enforcement powers. Second, the licensing officials may be committed to the existing policy in their states or may be eager to try another approach to regulating homes. Third, the number of regulated homes has not increased dramatically in the past few years, despite the large number of registered homes in states like Texas and Michigan, and despite the influence of the Child Care Food Program nationwide. Rather, increases have been localized in certain states and under certain regulatory systems.

States, Family Day Care Regulatory Policy, and Number of Family Day Care Providers

State	Current Regulation	Children Covered by Policy (including own children)	Number of Providers
Alabama	License	1–6°	2500
Alaska	License	4–10	350
Arizona	None, except for public $$	None, for fewer than 5	1500 "Certified"
Arkansas	License	6–10	430
California	License	1–6	23,500
Colorado	License	1–6	8330
Connecticut	License	1–4	2400
Delaware	License	1–6	480
Dist. of Columbia	License	1–5°	670
Florida	License (optional w/county)	1–5	1270
Georgia	Register (voluntary)	3–6	1000
Hawaii	License	2–5	280
Idaho	License	1–6	250
Illinois	License	3–8	8600
Indiana	License	1–10	1600
Iowa	Register (voluntary)	1–6	2600

State	Current Regulation	Children Covered by Policy (including own children)	Number of Providers
Kansas	License and register (voluntary)	1–6 (R), 7–10 (L)	3900
Kentucky	License	4–12	215
Louisiana	None, except for public $$	None, for fewer than 6	80 "Certified"
Maine	License and register (mandatory)	3–12	530
Maryland	License	1–6	5200
Massachusetts	Register (mandatory)	1–6	5100
Michigan	Register (mandatory)	1–6	10,900
Minnesota	License	1–5	9000
Mississippi	License	6–15	100
Missouri	License	4–6°	500
Montana	Register (mandatory)	1–6	750
Nebraska	Register (mandatory)	1–8	1550
Nevada	License	5–6	50
New Hampshire	License	1–6	520
New Jersey	None, except for public $$	None, for fewer than 6	800 "Approved"
New Mexico	License	4–6	510
New York	License (called "certify")	1–6	6200
North Carolina	Register (no standards)	2–5°	130 "Certified"
North Dakota	License	1–7	1000
Ohio	None, except for public $$	None, for fewer than 4	20
Oklahoma	License	1–5	700
Oregon	Register (voluntary)	1–5	2100
Pennsylvania	Register (mandatory)	4–6°	1980
Puerto Rico	License	2–6	320
Rhode Island	License	1–6	1000
South Carolina	License (for public $$) and register (voluntary)	1–6	810
South Dakota	Register (both voluntary and mandatory)	1–12	2650
Tennessee	License	5–7°	300
Texas	Register (mandatory)	1–6°	14,250
Utah	License	3–6	1400

State	Current Regulation	Children Covered by Policy (including own children)	Number of Providers
Vermont	License	1–6	160
Virginia	License	5–9	260
Virgin Islands	License	3–6	10
Washington	License	1–6	7000
West Virginia	None, except for public $$	None, for fewer than 7	1150 "Approved"
Wisconsin	License	4–8	260
Wyoming	License (called "certify")	2–6	700

(°Does not include own children)
Totals:
States using licensing - 31
States using registration (mandatory) - 8
 registration (voluntary) - 3
States using both licensing and registration - 3
States where only regulation is for homes receiving public $$ - 5
Territories using licensing - 4

Appendix B:
Day Care Licensing: The Eroding Regulations

Earline D. Kendall
Lewis H. Walker

ABSTRACT: Day care licensing regulations are being eroded. State regulations are changing as the staff who oversee licensing at the state and local levels are cut and/or given responsibilities in addition to licensing. Nearly half the states are considering registration of day care homes. As part of Child Watch: Looking Out For America's Children, current licensing standards were examined and licensing offices of all states were queried concerning changes since 1980. The responses of 49 licensing offices are summarized. Professional assessment, as proposed by the National Association for the Education of Young Children, is suggested as an addition to licensing or registration.

A current, growing concern in the field of child care is the relationship between deregulation, licensing, registration, and voluntary assessment of day care programs. Deregulation as used in this report indicates policy changes and agency interpretations of policy which bring about diminution of day care regulation at the federal, state, and local levels. Licensing is the primary means of regulation currently operating and is controlled by the states. Registration is a mechanism used by the states for voluntary listing of family day homes. Assessment by professional groups provides programs with recognition for meeting standards beyond those required by licensing.

Distinctions between licensing, registration, and professional assessment are presented here to evaluate options that various states are considering as effects of deregulation become apparent. First, we provide a brief overview of the purpose of regulation and its historical significance. Then, we examine responses to questionnaires by 49 state licensing agencies and delineate the consequences of licensing changes. Finally, we suggest an addition to licensing: assessment by the profession to recognize programs that more than meet licensing standards.

Historical Overview of Regulation

Licensing of day care programs, for the most part, has served to provide a safety level of protection for young children while they were away from their families. Morgan (1977) suggested that licensing defined a "floor of quality" (p. 23). Licensing provided a means of "regulating" those programs that were inspected for health and fire code compliance and met a diffuse set of guidelines laid out by day care licensing agents of the various states. Licensing regulations have usually been couched in terms of *minimum,* or least acceptable, standards, usually reflecting a philosophy of preventing harm to children in day care rather than providing exemplary care for children.

While there has been a lack of consensus of, and even criticism of, government policy regulating day care, even the harshest critics agree that "children's health and safety should be safeguarded by some public regulator body" (Orton & Langham, 1980, p. 47). Beyond the issues of health and safety there is little conformity of content or form in states' delineation of day care standards, even though day care professionals readily acknowledge that day care involves much more than health and safety factors. All 50 states have day care licensing standards, but states vary widely in their levels of specificity and sophistication. An example of the wide variation in standards is the strict adherence to detailed sanitation standards by some states, while other states merely mention that sufficient toilet and lavatory facilities shall be available.

In order to interpret meaningfully the results of the present licensing survey, an overview of the historical development of day care licensing is in order. The purposes and significance of day care licensing emerge from even a cursory study of the development of day care regulation. The purpose that regulation serves is that of providing minimal safety standards in order to prevent harm to children who are cared for in day care settings. Compared to other educational or social programs, regulation came late to day care.

The social and policy forces important to day care historically include the importance of family privacy, rights of families related to their children, and the welfare tradition of day care. By 1920, most states had some form of regulation for institutions providing foster care for children. Following World War II, state standards governing institutional care of children were expanded or appended to include children in day care. The effort to modify these standards was hurried, and often the result was less than appropriate for day care needs (Class, 1980).

During the late 1960s and early 1970s, when federal funding for child care was plentiful, Federal Interagency Day Care Requirements (FIDCR) were instituted to ensure adequate standards for those programs using federal funds. FIDCR reflected the need for uniform standards across federal programs and pointed to the lack of uniformity in state standards. Since a solid national consensus did not emerge, FIDCR standards went unenforced from the time of their inception in 1968 (Zigler & Heller, 1980). The moratorium on compliance centered on staff-child ratios, with the cost of care a central question (Morgan, 1980). The efforts to implement FIDCR reflected the belief among many early childhood professionals that regulations which demanded high standards could ensure quality care. Some, however, feared that federal standards could inhibit states and local communities from setting higher standards; destroy cultural differences of program philosophies; professionalize child rearing, undermining parents; result in excessive monitoring and increase costs of care (Morgan, 1977, pp. 24–25).

In an effort to ensure enforcement of some regulation for federal programs, in addition to what state licensing required, compromises in FIDCR were attempted. The "new" rules were actually a relaxation of standards regarding staff-child ratios,[1] social services, and parent participation (Friedman, 1980; Lynn, 1980). Although consensus could not be found for the compromise version of FIDCR, these relaxed standards were implemented for federally funded programs. Finally, in 1981, the regulations were eliminated (Adams, 1982).

A clear need for some form of regulation was apparent despite the fact these regulations were inadequate from the beginning and failed at the implementation stage. Increasing numbers of young children were cared for outside their own homes. Children were placed in group settings at younger and younger ages. A growing number of young children were in single parent homes, requiring the services of child care providers who were not family members.

At the very time when day care needs escalated, a policy trend toward decentralized and deregulated government involvement occurred. This trend affected the regulation of child care. Deregulation of child care failed to encounter much notice or resistance, because the professional community was struggling with funding cutbacks and the cancellation of programs. Deregulation of child care prompted little notice by the public because of the broader effort of minimizing government control in areas that are traditionally under private control. Americans generally consider their children to be beyond the reach of outside agencies, except for public education; therefore, many parents wish to maintain their right to select child care without interference from government control.

At the same time that FIDCR proponents admitted failure, states began systematic efforts to deregulate day care licensing. Since most efforts at enforcement of state regulations occurred already at the local rather than the state or federal level, further decentralization of day care licensing hardly seemed possible.

The move, then, toward deregulation of day care programs met with little public resistance. The apparent apathy, in part, stemmed from informal selection practices by most parents (Grotberg, 1980). The National Day Care Home Study (NDCHS) (Fosburg, 1981) found that of an estimated 1.3 million day care homes, only 137,865 of them were regulated. In subsequent analyses of these data, Stevens (1982) noted that 94% of the 5 million children in family day care in 1975 were in unregulated care. These findings are consistent with the Bush Institute estimates (Adams, 1982).

Recognizing the problem of parents' informal arrangements, critics have proposed a variety of solutions in addition to registration of homes: parental education (Travis & Perrault, 1980), greater attention to fair implementation of licensing requirements (Diamond, 1982), and a call for a national policy on children (Hoffman, 1980). Appropriate licensing and enforcement of regulation, it is argued, will provide parents with a ready means of distinguishing good care from merely custodial or mediocre care.

Thrust of Child Watch Project

In the climate of deregulation that increased during the 10-year period that FIDCR was debated at the national level, states also showed a marked tendency toward leniency in both enforcement and the statement of specifics in licensing standards. In an effort to monitor the extent of changes, this study asked each state licensing agency to submit a copy of current day care standards and to respond to questions concerning licensing changes since 1980. This survey was part of a larger effort initiated by Children's Defense Fund through the project Child Watch: Looking Out for America's Children. Child Watch incorporated the efforts of ten national organizations[2] in monitoring at local levels the effects of policy changes and budget cutbacks affecting child care. Providers, parents, and knowledgeable community resource persons were contacted by Child Watch volunteers in 1982 in numerous areas of the country for documentation concerning changes in child care. As a part of the Children's Defense Fund study, 50 states, two territories, and the District of Columbia were queried about their current status in regulating child care. Forty-six states, the Virgin Islands, Puerto Rico, and the District of Columbia responded. The present report synthesizes state licensing standards and licensing changes noted by respondents.

Procedures

A letter was sent to each state licensing agency requesting responses to questions concerning their licensing changes since 1980. Along with the questionnaire (Table 1) went a request for a copy of current licensing standards. Questions focused on: number of centers licensed, number of homes regulated, and applications pending; licensing changes since 1980 and proposed changes; staff work load changes; and numbers and types of complaints received at the state level regarding child care. A follow-up letter was sent to those states not responding within three weeks. These requests elicited 49 responses from the 53 contacts. Attempts were made to reach the four states which had not responded by mail and by telephone.

Table 1

Licensing Questionnaire
CHILD WATCH

Name_____   State_____

Title_____

1. Has there been any change in the number of complaints received by the licensing agency from parents and the community over the last several years?_____ over the past six months?_____

   Has there been any change in the nature of the complaints?_____
   Briefly describe:

   Are data compiled on the types and numbers of complaints and the disposition of those complaints?_____

2. Has there been any change in the licensing staff over the past year?
   _____ over the past six months?_____

3. Has there been any change in the work load over the past year?_____
   over the past six months?_____
   Describe briefly:

4. How many centers are now licensed?_____
   How many additional applications are pending?_____

5. How many homes are now regulated?_____
   How many applications are pending?_____

6. Have there been changes in the licensing requirements for centers since 1980?_____Family day care homes?_____
   Describe these changes (include quality changes--weaker or improved):

7. Are any changes in licensing requirements being proposed through currently filed legislation or being considered by your agency?_____
   Please describe:

Results

Number of Centers Licensed

The total number of licensed centers reported was 44,457 with an additional 3,537 licenses pending. Table 2 delineates the number in each state. From an examination of Table 2, it can be noted that the range in the number of licensed centers is from 20 (Virgin Islands) to 4,800 (Texas), with a mean of 941.

The total number of homes regulated was 151,990, with an additional 5,861 licenses pending. California (26,859), Michigan (10,322), Texas (14,837), and Washington (10,500) are the states indicating the largest numbers of regulated homes. Registration is available in California, Texas, and Michigan. Of the four states with the largest numbers of homes regulated, only Washington has licensing without registration.

TABLE 2: State Responses

	Number of Centers	Regulation of Day Care Homes	Number of Homes
Alabama	890	Licensing	2527
Alaska	109	Licensing	348
Arizona	645 *	None	1332
Arkansas	858	Licensing	465
California	4596	Licensing	26859
Colorado	600 *	Licensing	8333 *
Connecticut		Licensing	2400
Delaware	121	Licensing	510 *
District of Columbia	250	Licensing	299
Florida	3236	Licensing	1325
Georgia	1350	Voluntary	1284
Hawaii	299	Licensing	311
Idaho #		Licensing	
Illinois	2254	Licensing	8372
Indiana	654	Licensing	5000
Iowa	953	Voluntary	2567
Kansas #		Optional	3930
Kentucky	700 *	Licensing	225 *
Louisiana #		None	
Maine	116	Optional	512
Maryland	721	Licensing	5200
Massachusetts	1500 *	Registration	5100 *
Michigan	2289	Registration	10322
Minnesota	907	Licensing	9010
Mississippi #		Licensing	
Missouri	525	Licensing	1027
Montana	125	Registration	600
Nebraska	208	Registration	1545
Nevada	36	Licensing	9
New Hampshire	475	Licensing	524
New Jersey	1500	None	None
New Mexico	373	Licensing	217
New York	800 *	Licensing	6230
North Carolina	2206	Registration	6000
North Dakota	128	Licensing	878
Ohio	2000	None	N/A
Oklahoma	885	Licensing	712
Oregon	463	Registration	2229
Pennsylvania	1086	Registration	2304
Rhode Island	70	Licensing	800
South Carolina	1000 *	Optional	1020 *
South Dakota	75	Registration	800 *
Tennessee	1222	Licensing	502
Texas	4800 **	Registration	14837
Utah	138	Licensing	1500 *
Vermont	102	Licensing	160
Virginia	582	Licensing	153
Washington	1055	Licensing	10500
West Virginia	140	None	2295
Wisconsin	990	Licensing	270
Wyoming	300	Licensing	600 *
Puerto Rico	105	Licensing	42
Virgin Islands	20	Licensing	5
Totals	44,457		151,990

* Approximations

** Does not include 1200 + half-day programs

Information not received from state agencies

NA Information not available

Changes in Licensing Since 1980

Thirty-four states reported changes in licensing requirements since 1980. Several states specified that changes were minor amendments for the purpose of clarification; however, the majority of states reporting changes list substantial additions or deletions to the licensing code.

Changes which respondents characterized as improvements include the following: in the area of staff requirements—staffing pattern improved, staff qualifications strengthened, staff/child ratios bettered, and staff training added; in the area of health and safety—fire extinguisher or smoke alarm required in homes, TB test for applicants, transportation (use of seatbelts), and swimming pools regulated; in the area of requirements for directors—age for operators and directors raised to 21, and experience required for operators; in the area of nutrition—improvements noted in menu planning; in the area of enforcement of regulations—$100-per-day fines, financial accountability to the department imposed, affidavit and fingerprint check, report of criminal conviction, mandatory enforcement of abuse/neglect cases. States noted improvements with specific results such as the saving of family day home regulation and consumer education programs, the addition of infant regulations in four states, school age regulations in two, and making state requirements correspond to the proposed FIDCR. Six states indicated a change to include voluntary registration of family day homes.

Changes that were characterized by respondents as negative included: eliminating routine monitoring, implementing a 3-year license as opposed to the 2-year license that had been in effect, more specificity in regulations (and therefore "nitpicking" reported), temporary reverting to 1971 standards due to litigation, elimination of after school "tolerance for ratios," omission of infant, toddler, and standards for older children, pressure for weakening standards in order to cut cost of care.

Proposed Changes

Thirty-one states have proposed changes. Often changes suggested are for the purpose of improving definitions used or making language or changes coincide with other departments' changes. Other proposals include standards for programs serving handicapped children.

A number of changes relate to exemptions; specific exemptions suggested are military base programs, church sponsored programs, primarily educational programs, Title XX and IV-A programs, employer provided child care, and food brought from home. Four states are proposing registration of family day homes. On-site directors and stronger training and experience requirements for directors are proposed. Two states mentioned a relaxation of staff/child ratios. Others proposed raising the licensing fee and moving to a biennial (from an annual) license.

Complaints Received

In some states, records of complaints related to licensing are not kept at the state level; however, 30 of the 49 respondents indicated an increase in the number of complaints logged since 1980 as compared with the years preceding 1980. Only 15 agencies indicated no change in the number of complaints noted. These 15 did not report a lack of complaints, but merely no increase in the number of complaints. The source of complaints was not solicited in the questionnaire.

A marked increase in complaints relating to abuse, neglect, and inappropriate treatment was reported by 28 of the 49 states responding. Thirteen mentioned abuse, four particularly specifying sexual abuse in centers and family day homes in both licensed and unlicensed facilities. Ten linked the rise in number of complaints to lack of supervision and to instances of actual child neglect. Five noted inappropriate discipline, treatment, and punishment as problems.

Complaints concerning staff/child ratio were mentioned by seven respondents. These seven responses were tied to the above abuse-neglect-inappropriate treatment complaints.

Change in Staff and Workload

All respondents answered questions on staff changes and workload. Of the 49 respondents, 36 reported changes in licensing staff during the past year; 41 indicated changes in workloads.

More programs monitored by fewer licensing staff was the most often noted workload change. Changes in workloads in several cases included added responsibilities other than day care licensing.

Changes include vacancies due to budget reduction, retirements and resignations without replacement, and a freeze on hiring. Other workload changes include legislative program modifications, agency reorganization, and a shift from contracted service to agency service.

Discussion

Several problem areas are immediately evident in surveying current standards, recent changes, and proposed legislation. Although some positive changes are occurring (e.g., four states are adding infant regulations), such changes vary from state to state and few consistent positive patterns emerge, while the erosion of standards is clearly consistent throughout responses. Repeatedly, respondents noted reductions in staff, additional staff responsibilities, low priority of day care, lowering of staff-child ratios, and the replacement of the licensing of family day homes with self-registration. In view of the fact that family day care homes outnumber day care centers three to one, the move toward self-registration of homes rather than licensing is a significant change.

Exemption of military-based programs and church-related programs is under consideration in three states. The National Council of Churches reported a survey (Preschool Education, 1982) sent to 68,000 congregations. Of the 27,000 responses, 12,077 indicated that they had child care under church-sponsored programs. California, one of the states currently considering church exemption, licenses the second largest number of programs in the nation. Because significant numbers of these programs exist under church sponsorship, strong opposition to church exemption is expected.

A particular problem in examining licensing standards is the lack of consensus on nomenclature. Comparisons of specific state regulations is difficult because either terms are different or the same terms have different meanings across states. The variation in terms used may account for the significant difference in the number of "centers" reported here (44,000) and the number reported in the National Day Care

Study (18,300) (Abt, 1978). The period since the National Day Care Study is concurrent with the period where increased employment of women dramatically extended the need for child care. We speculate that there has been some increase in the number of day care programs; however, this increase hardly explains the more than twice as many centers reported four years after the National Day Care Study.

Increase in sexual abuse complaints can be attributed to increased awareness on the part of parents and the public, and to increased tensions as economic hard times affect children, but neither fully explains the "250% increase in complaints" stated by one respondent. While sexual abuse and neglect of children in licensed centers and homes is being reported in nine states, deregulation or diminishing effectiveness of the licensing process is also occurring.

An obvious regulation change is the change from licensing to registration. Adams (1982b), in reporting the Bush Institute findings on the National Survey of Family Day Care Regulations, found that 25 states have some proposed day care legislation pending (or enacted this session), and nine states are currently undertaking a comprehensive examination of day care in the state. If the states who are considering registration and/or have registration legislation pending pass these regulations within the next year, half the states may register homes (Adams, 1982b). Proponents of registration view voluntary registration primarily as a means of raising awareness of good care; on the other side, registration may be seen as "better than nothing."

In states that have mounted a massive public education campaign, such as Texas, the result is a large increase in the number of providers who are now "on the rolls." Virginia failed to implement registration due to a lack of public acceptance that caused the state to return to licensing. Registration of homes where licensing is mandatory requires a change in statute. The penalty for failure to register is a misdemeanor in some states, with a fine of $50 per day; Connecticut has increased the fine to $100 a day. In Texas, a heavily funded media blitz, emphasizing the registration regulation and fine for failure to register, raised awareness of both parents and providers for the need of regulated child care. Tennessee indicated that allocations for such a campaign must be included if registration is to be instituted successfully.

Registration provides for self-evaluation of fire, safety, and environmental conditions, which means attesting to such items as smoke detectors and fire extinguishers. Where licensing of homes is in effect, licensing counselors inspect for these items. Registration provides for random home visits to check for compliance (Sales, 1980). A major issue in the registration versus licensing dilemma is the number of children in a program. Registration appears to be one means of holding on to the principle of licensing at a time when deregulation threatens the licensing concept.

Powell (1980) voiced concerns of the child care profession about the need for standards within the profession. The National Association for the Education of Young Children (NAEYC) is similarly concerned and is proposing endorsement of programs meeting more than basic licensing standards. Under their proposal, licensed providers would seek evaluation voluntarily. At a time when states have various options for regulating child care or for even abandoning regulations altogether, a move by the child care profession toward self-regulation could upgrade child care and the profession as well. Both child care and the child care profession are in dire need of upgrading. Self-regulation is a move to improve the quality of care offered children while enhancing the image of the child care profession. Professional credentialing by trained validators would provide parents a means of discerning which programs offer a program of high quality as opposed to those that are licensed or registered only. At its best, day care regulation has been a means of assuring that certain minimal standards are met. Voluntary professional accreditation can go a step beyond and ascertain the level of compliance a program has with higher standards.

Licensing and the need for standards reached its zenith with the fight for FIDCR. When those regulations proved to be unenforceable, the licensing effort lost ground. Registration may prove to be "better than nothing," as one licensing agent said, but that seems too little to offer. Self-regulation by the day care profession appears to fill an increasing need. In a field that at best is monitored poorly, the regulation of programs for young children is a concern that conscientiously cannot be ignored.

Footnotes

1. With the exception of ratios for infant and toddler care.
2. National Organizations/Child Watch: Church Women United, United Methodist Church, Lutheran Church in America, Young Women's Christian Association, National Council of Negro Women, National Association for the Education of Young Children, League of United Latin American Citizens, Southern Rural Women's Network, Council of Jewish Federations, and Association of Junior Leagues.

References

Abt Associates. (1978). National day care study: Preliminary findings and their implications. Cambridge, MA: Author.

Adams, D. (1982a). Family day care regulations: State policies in transition. *Day Care Journal*, Summer.

Adams, D. (1982b). *Summary of findings: National survey of family day care regulations.* Bush Institute for Child and Family Policy: The University of North Carolina at Chapel Hill.

Appropriateness of the federal interagency day care requirements: Report of findings and recommendations. (1978). Washington, DC: HEW.

Class, N.E. (1980). Development of child day care facility licensing. In S. Kilmer (Ed.), *Advances in early education and day care: A research annual.* Greenwich, CT: JAI Press.

Diamond, F. (1982). *The child care handbook: Needs, programs, and possibilities.* Washington, DC: CDF.

Fosburg, S. (1981). *Family day care in the United States: Summary of Findings.* Final Report of National Day Care Home Study. Washington, DC: U.S. Department of Health and Human Services (DHHS Publication No. (OHDS) 80-30282).

Friedman, D. T. (1980). Summary of new day care regulations. *Day Care and Early Education, 8,* (2), 31+.

Grotberg, E.H. (1980). The roles of the federal government in child care. In S. Kilmer (Ed.), *Advances in early education and day care: A research annual,* Greenwich, CT: JAI Press.

Hoffman, E. (1980). A national policy for children—How do we get there? In R. Haskins & J.J. Gallagher (Eds.), *Care and education of young children in America: Policy, politics and social science.* Norwood, NJ: Ablex.

Lynn, J. (1980). Compromise standards issued by HEW. *Day Care and Early Education, 7,* (4), 13+.

Morgan, G. (1980). Federal day care requirements: One more round. *Day Care and Early Education, 8,* (2), 26-30+.

Morgan, G. G. (1977). Federal day care standards in content. In *Policy issued in day care: Summaries of 21 papers* (prepared for the U.S. Department of Health, Education, and Welfare Contract No. 100-77-0017). Washington, DC: Center for Systems and Program Development.

Orton, R. E. & Langham, B. (1980). What is government's role in quality day care? In S. Kilmer (Ed.), *Advances in early education and day care: A research annual.* Greenwich, CT: JAI Press.

Powell, D. R. (1980). *Toward a sociological perspective of relation between parents' and child care programs.* In S. Kilmer (Ed.), *Advances in early education and day care: A research annual.* Greenwich, CT: JAI Press.

Ruopp, R. R. & Travers, J. (1982). Janus faces day care: Perspectives on quality and cost. In E. F. Zigler & E. W. Gordon (Eds.), *Day care: Scientific and social policy issues.* Boston, MA: Auburn House.

Sale, J. S. (1980). Family day care: The registration controversy. *Day Care and Early Education,* Fall, 10-14.

Stevens, J. H., Jr. (1982). The national day care home study: Family day care in the United States. *Young Children, 37,* (4), 59-66.

Surveys to document churches' role in day care. (1982). *Report on Preschool Education, 14* (12), 3.

Travis, N. E. & Perreault, N. (1980). Day care as a resource to families. In L. G. Katz (Ed.), *Current topics in early childhood education,* (Vol. III). Norwood, NJ: Ablex.

Zigler, E. & Heller, K. A. (1980). Day care standards approach critical juncture. *Day Care and Early Education, 7,* (3), 7-8.

Zigler, E. F. & Gordon, E. W. (1982). *Day care: Scientific and social policy issues.* Boston, MA: Auburn House.

Appendix C:
Selected Agencies and Organizations Concerned with Day Care

The following list of agencies and organizations contains those most frequently mentioned in the professional literature in the field of day care. This list is not totally inclusive as there are numerous organizations involved to some extent with child care. An explanation of purpose, as well as names and addresses of additional groups, may be found in the article "Who's Who in Child Care: The Organizations," by Helen Blank, in *Child Care Information Exchange* (August 1984).

American Home Economics Association (AHEA)
2010 Massachusetts Ave., N.W.
Washington, DC 20036
(202) 862-8300
Produces information on education and nutrition.

American Parents Committee (APC)
1346 Connecticut Ave., N.W.
Washington, DC 20036
(202) 785-3169
Supports legislation relating to children and families; a division of the Child Welfare League of America.

American Red Cross (ARC)
17th and D Sts., N.W.
Washington, DC 20006
(202) 737-8300
Publishes information on nursing and health services.

Association for Childhood Education International (ACEI)
11141 Georgia Ave., Suite 200
Wheaton, MD 20902
(301) 942-2443
Promotes, through state and local groups, educational practices; conducts workshops and conferences and publishes many materials.

Children's Defense Fund (CDF)
122 C St., N.W.

Washington, DC 20001
(202) 628-8787
Acts as an advocate of the nation's children in all areas including day care; active in litigation and legislation; publishes newsletters, handbooks, and books.

Family Service Association of America (FSAA)
44 E. 23rd St.
New York, NY 10010
(212) 674-6100
Publishes informational materials on parent-child relationships and other problems of family living; provides family counseling.

National Association for the Education of Young Children (NAEYC)
1834 Connecticut Ave., N.W.
Washington, DC 20009
(202) 232-8777
Focuses on the provision of educational services and resources; publishes a journal, books, brochures, and posters; sponsors the "Week of the Young Child."

National Committee for Citizens in Education (NCCE)
Wide Lake Village Green, Suite 410
Columbia, MD 21044
(301) 997-9300
Promotes parent participation in educational issues; conducts research; publishes newsletters, handbooks, and pamphlets.

Parents Without Partners (PWP)
7910 Woodmont Ave., Suite 1000
Bethesda, MD 20814
(301) 654-8850
Participates in research on the single parent in order to help alleviate problems related to parenting; maintains a speakers bureau; sponsors conventions and several publications.

Subject Index

Compiled by Linda Webster